TOP GRADE
ENGLISH

GEOFF BARTON ◆ MATTHEW BERRY ◆ JANE CHRISTOPHER

*And tear our pleasures
with rough strife
Through the iron
gates of life*

Vladimir: (*hurt, coldly*) May one enquire where his Highn...

Estragon: In a ditch.

Vladimir: (*admiringly*) A ditch! Where?

OXFORD
UNIVERSITY PRESS

OXFORD
UNIVERSITY PRESS

Great Clarendon Street, Oxford OX2 6DP

Oxford University Press is a department of the University of Oxford.
It furthers the University's objective of excellence in research, scholarship,
and education by publishing worldwide in

Oxford New York

Athens Auckland Bangkok Bogotá Buenos Aires
Calcutta Cape Town Chennai Dar es Salaam Delhi
Florence Hong Kong Istanbul Karachi Kuala Lumpur
Madrid Melbourne Mexico City Mumbai Nairobi Paris
São Paulo Singapore Taipei Tokyo Toronto Warsaw

and associated companies in Berlin Ibadan

Oxford is a registered trade mark of Oxford University Press
in the UK and in certain other countries

Top Grade English
© Geoff Barton, Matthew Berry and Jane Christopher 1999
Published by Oxford University Press 1999

A CIP catalogue record for this book is available from
the British Library

ISBN 0 19 831446 9

Designed by Ian Foulis & Associates, Plympton, Plymouth, PL7 1RQ
Printed by Butler & Tanner, Frome

Top Grade English

Introduction

Who you are

Top Grade English is written specifically for the most able students at GCSE.

You may be in Year 10 or Year 11. You may be following one of a variety of syllabuses. You may be in a state or an independent school. But you will already have an exceptional ability in English.

As we wrote the book, we had a clear view of whom we were writing for, based on our experience as practising English teachers. We see you as someone who probably enjoys English, someone who has strong ideas and feelings, someone who can express themselves with precision in speech and writing. We imagine that like you reading. We know that you have a sharp mind. And we suspect you get bored by textbooks which patronize you or attempt merely to entertain you with time-filling activities.

Therefore we've kept you at the centre of the book with texts, resources and activities which will give you the essential skills to gain Grade A or A* in English. We imagine at the start of the process that you may be working somewhere around Grade B or B+, but with the very clear potential to gain the top grades in English and English Literature.

Structure

Each unit of the book is built progressively. We start by mapping out the study skills you will need, and then guide you quickly through them. The units are shaped to stretch your understanding and skills through the use of challenging and sometimes provocative extracts.

We've tried to keep our text to a minimum so you won't have large amounts of editorial to plough through. Instead, we wanted to give you a clear picture of what you'll need to be able to do if you are to achieve the highest grades.

Some of the units are specifically built around coursework activities. Others are examination-focused. This structure is based on the requirements of the main examination boards. We also give you skills and reference sections: an introduction to the reading and writing skills you'll most need to develop, plus advice on working under pressure in examinations, understanding texts from other literary periods, and background information on writers.

Speaking and listening are also essential GCSE skills. You'll probably already be a talented user of spoken English and, we imagine, a good listener. We've included opportunities for speaking and listening throughout the book, but placed particular emphasis on reading and writing, because here is where you'll gather most of your final marks.

Who we are

We all teach English, two of us in state schools, one in an independent school. For two terms we all taught together at a large, highly-successful comprehensive school in York, and there we decided that our most able students needed a textbook to themselves. So this is it and we hope you enjoy using it.

It is intended to do more than help you notch up examination success, though we're naturally keen that you should gain top grades. We also want it to lead you into interesting new areas of English work, which cannot always be fully explored in class, and to provide you with excellent foundations if you choose to go on to study English at Advanced Level or beyond.

Geoff Barton
Matthew Berry
Jane Christopher

Contents

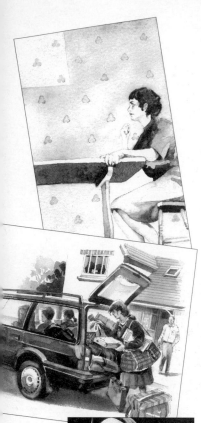

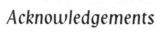

Reading Skills

This unit demonstrates the reading skills you need to gain top grades in English at GCSE and as preparation for study of English at A-level.

A* candidates need to be able to do more than read and understand texts. They need to read with real subtlety. This means spotting implications, hints, and meanings that lurk beneath the surface. They need to have a sharp sense of the way writers present characters, settings, and themes, and be able to use a variety of reading strategies in this process. They also need to be very attuned to language and be able to identify the features that give different types of texts or genres their distinctive qualities.

Study Skills

- Analysing written texts – skimming, scanning, explaining key words, summarizing main ideas
- Reading beneath the surface of texts
- Being able to identify the language features of different genres (for example, crime fiction, and journalism)

Higher Order Reading Skills

The main skills involved in higher level reading are:
- Skimming – reading a text quickly to pick up the gist of it
- Scanning – reading text quickly to find a specific idea or point
- Identifying key words
- Summarizing main ideas

Certain texts lend themselves more than others to advanced reading skills. Information texts often use visual signals to help readers find their way about. These signals might include:
- Organization by alphabetical order
- Headings and subheadings
- Bold text, underlining, or italics to make key ideas stand out

Activity

Page 7 shows an extract from a Dictionary of Science.
1   Before reading it, look at the questions below and on page 8. Then work as quickly as you can using the reading skills listed above. Aim to complete the task in 60 seconds.

Scanning questions:
- What is DAT?
- How fast does digital recording sample the pressure of sound waves each second?

Dictionary of Science

digestive system the mouth, stomach, intestine, and associated glands of animals, which are responsible for digesting food. The food is broken down by physical and chemical means in the stomach; digestion is completed, and most nutrients are absorbed in the small intestine; what remains is stored and concentrated into faeces in the large intestine. See gut.

In smaller, simpler animals such as jellyfishes, the digestive system is simply a cavity (coelenteron or enteric cavity) with a 'mouth' into which food is taken; the digestive portion is dissolved and absorbed in this cavity, and the remains are ejected back through the mouth.

digit in mathematics, and of the numbers from 0 to 9 in the decimal system. Different bases have different ranges of digits. For example, the hexadecimal system has digits 0 to 9 and A to F, whereas the binary system has two digits (or bits), 0 and 1.

digital in electronics and computing, a term meaning 'coded as numbers'. A digital system uses two-state, either on/off or high/low voltage pulses, to encode, receive, and transmit information. A *digital display* shows discrete values as numbers (as opposed to an analogue signal, such as the continuous sweep of a pointer on a dial).

Digital electronics is the technology that underlies digital techniques. Low-power, miniature, integrated circuits (chips) provide the means for the coding, storage, transmission, processing, and reconstruction of information of all kinds.

digital audio tape (DAT) digitally recorded audio tape produced in cassettes that can carry two hours of sound on each side and are about half the size of standard cassettes. DAT players/recorders were developed 1987 but not marketed in the UK until 1989. Prerecorded cassettes are copyprotected. The first DAT for computer data was produced in 1988.

DAT machines are constructed like video cassette recorders (though they use metal audio tape), with a movable playback head, the tape winding in a spiral around a rotating drum. The tape can also carry additional information; for example, it can be programmed to skip a particular track and repeat another. The music industry delayed releasing prerecorded DAT cassettes because of fears of bootlegging, but a system has now been internationally agreed whereby it is not possible to make more than one copy of any prerecorded compact disc or DAT. DAT is mainly used in recording studios for making master tapes. The system was developed by Sony.

By 1990, DATs for computer data had been developed to a capacity of around 2.5 gigabytes per tape, achieved by using helical scan recording (in which the tape covers some 90% of the total head area of the rotating drum). This enables data from the tape to be read over 200 times faster than it can be written. Any file can be located within 60 seconds.

digital compact cassette (DCC) digitally recorded audio cassette that is roughly the same size as a standard cassette. It cannot be played on a normal tape recorder, though standard tapes can be played on a DCC machine; this is known as 'backwards compatibility'. The playing time is 90 minutes.

A DCC player has a stationary playback and recording head similar to that in ordinary tape decks, though the tape used is chrome video tape. The cassettes are copy-protected and can be individually programmed for playing order. Some DCC decks have a liquid-crystal digital-display screen, which can show track titles and other information encoded on the tape. DCC machines were launched in the UK in 1992, with some 500 prerecorded tapes to go with them. The system was developed by Philips.

digital computer computing device that operates on a two-state system, using symbols that are internally coded as binary numbers (numbers made up of combinations of the digits 0 and 1); see computer.

digital data transmission in computing, a way of sending data by converting all signals (whether pictures, sounds, or words) into numeric (normally binary) codes before transmission, then reconverting them on receipt. This virtually eliminates any distortion or degradation of the signal during transmission, storage, or processing.

digital recording technique whereby the pressure of sound waves is sampled more than 30,000 times a second and the values converted by computer into precise numerical values. These are recorded and, during playback, are reconverted to sound waves.

This technique gives very high-quality reproduction. The numerical values converted by computer represent the original sound-wave form exactly and are recorded on compact disc. When this is played back by laser, the exact values are retrieved. When the signal is fed via an amplifier to a loudspeaker, sound waves exactly like the original ones are reproduced.

digital sampling electronic process used in telecommunications for transforming a constantly varying (analogue) signal into one composed of discrete units, a digital signal. In the creation of recorded music, sampling enables the composer, producer, or remix engineer to borrow discrete vocal or instrumental parts from other recorded work (it is also possible to sample live sound).

A telephone microphone changes sound waves into an analogue signal that fluctuates up and down like a wave. In the digitizing process the waveform is sampled thousands of times a second and each part of the sampled wave is given a binary code number (made up of combinations of the digits 0 and 1) related to the height of the wave at that point, which is transmitted along the telephone line. Using digital signals, messages can be transmitted quickly, accurately, and economically.

- Is the number 11 a digit?
- What is backwards compatibility?

2   Once you have completed the activity, think about:

- How you approached the task. How did you try to find the required information?
- Which questions proved most straightforward?

All of the above questions tested your scanning skills – searching a text for specific points of information.

1   Now look more closely at the dictionary entry about digital audio tape. Imagine that you are going to be tested on your knowledge of this information. Arrange it into a page of notes (one side of A4 paper maximum) which:

- shows the key points in the development of DAT
- uses visual signals to help you to organize the information – underlining key words, arrows, capital letters, etc.
- uses the note-making format that you find most useful (see examples given below)

2   Then compare with a partner:

- which information from the extract you retained
- which information you cut
- points where you simplified the text
- points where you used the text directly from the extract
- how you organized your notes
- specific visual signals you used to highlight certain key points

3   Now based on your notes, if you had to say what was the single most important point to make about the development of DAT, what would you say?

Mind Mapping

Everyone makes notes in slightly different ways. Some people like to use diagrams; some like text to dominate; some like spider diagrams; some prefer bullet points and lists. Choose a format that will be most successful for you.

Now take the notes you wrote for question 1 above and try to present them visually. Work quickly (three minutes maximum).

Linear and Non-linear Texts

Some texts are easier than others to interrogate for precise information in this way. Encyclopaedia and reference books have been written to help the reader locate information quickly. This is non-linear information – that is, in general the text is not a narrative, with one point leading to the next as it would in a short story, newspaper report or recipe.

Sometimes, for interest, non-fiction writers use linear formats to add human interest to information. In the *Hutchinson Dictionary of Science*, for example, the discovery of the human digestive system is presented in narrative form, giving the tone of the text a different feel.

Hutchinson Dictionary of Science: Digestive System

GREAT EXPERIMENTS AND DISCOVERIES

An army marches on its stomach

On 6 June 1822 at Fort Mackinac, Michigan, USA, an 18-year-old French Canadian was accidentally wounded in the abdomen by the discharge of musket. He was brought to the army surgeon, US physician William Beaumont (1785-1853), who noted several serious wounds and, in particular, a hole in the abdominal wall and stomach. The surgeon observed that through this hole the patient 'was pouring out the food he had taken for breakfast.'

The patient, Alexis St Martin, a trapper by profession, was serving with the army as a porter and general servant. Not surprisingly, St Martin was at first unable to keep food in his stomach. As the wound gradually healed, firm dressings were needed to retain the stomach contents. Beaumont tended his patient assiduously and tried during the ensuing months to close the hole in his stomach, without success. After 18 months, a small, protruding fleshy fold had grown to fill the aperture (fistula). This 'valve' could be opened simply by pressing it with a finger.

Digestion… inside and out

At this point, it occurred to Beaumont that here was an ideal opportunity to study the process of digestion. His patient must have been an extremely tough character to have survived the accident at all. For the next nine years he was the subject of a remarkable series of pioneering experiments, in which Beaumont was able to vary systematically the conditions under which digestion took place and discover the chemical principles involved.

Beaumont attacked the problem of digestion in two ways. He studied how substances were actually digested in the stomach, and also how they were 'digested' outside the stomach in the digestive juices he extracted from St Martin. He found it was easy enough to drain out the juices from his patient 'by placing the subject on his left side, depressing the valve within the aperture, introducing a gum elastic tube and then turning him… on introducing the tube the fluid soon began to run.'

Beaumont was basically interested in the rate and temperature of digestion, and also the chemical conditions that favoured different stages of the process of digestion. He describes a typical experiment (he performed hundreds), where (a) digestion in the stomach is contrasted (b) with artificial digestion in glass containers kept at suitable temperatures, like this:

(a) 'At 9 o'clock he breakfasted on bread, sausage and coffee, and kept exercising. 11 o'clock, 30 minutes, stomach two-thirds empty, aspects of weather similar, thermometer 298 (F), temperature of stomach 101 $1/_{28}$ and 100 $3/_{48}$. The appearance of contraction and dilation and alternative piston motions were distinctly observed at this examination. 12 o'clock, 20 minutes, stomach empty.

(b) 'February 7. At 8 o'clock, 30 minutes A.M. I put twenty grains of boiled codfish into three drachms of gastric juice and placed them on the bath. At 1 o'clock, 30 minutes, P.M., the fish in the gastric juice on the bath was almost dissolved, four grains only remaining; fluid opaque, white, nearly the colour of milk. 2 o'clock, the fish in the vial all completely dissolved.

All a matter of chemistry

Beaumont's research showed clearly for the first time just what happened during digestion and that digestion, as a process, could take place independently outside the body. He wrote that gastric juice: 'so far from being inert as water as some authors assert, is the most general solvent in nature of alimentary matter – even the hardest bone cannot withstand its action. It is capable, even out of the stomach, of effecting perfect digestion, with the aid of due and uniform degree of heat (100 degree Fahrenheit) and gentle agitation… I am impelled by the weight of evidence… to conclude that the change effected by it on the aliment, is *purely chemical*.'

Our modern understanding of the physiology of digestion as a process whereby foods are gradually broken down into their basic components follows logically from his work. An explanation of how the digestive juices flowed in the first place came in 1889, when Russian physiologist Ivan Pavlov (1849-1936) showed that their secretion in the stomach was controlled by the nervous system. By preventing the food eaten by a dog from actually entering the stomach, he found that the secretions of gastric juices began the moment the dog started eating, and continued as long as it did so. Since no food had entered the stomach, the secretions must be mediated by the nervous system.

Later it was found that the further digestion that takes place beyond the stomach was hormonally controlled. But it was Beamount's careful scientific work, which was published in 1933 with the title *Experiments and Observations on the Gastric Juice and Physiology of Digestion*, that triggered subsequent research in the field.

Scan the extract on page 9 for the specific points listed below. Then reflect on whether linear and non-linear texts call for different approaches when locating information.

- When was William Beaumont born?
- What was the profession of Alexis St Martin?
- What did Beaumont learn about how food is digested?
- What did Ivan Pavlov show?

Reading Beneath the Surface

At GCSE and A-level, the highest literature grades are awarded to students who can read beneath the surface level of texts. What does this mean in practice?

Writers can give us information about characters, places, and events directly and indirectly.

Read this opening of a short story by William Trevor, looking in particular at the way he presents the characters of Miss Smith and James Machen.

Miss Smith

One day Miss Smith asked James what a baby horse was called and James couldn't remember. He blinked and shook his head. He knew, he explained, but he just couldn't remember. Miss Smith said:

'Well, well, James Machen doesn't know what a baby horse is called.'

She said it loudly so that everyone in the classroom heard. James became very confused. He blinked and said:

'Pony, Miss Smith?'

'Pony! James Machen says a baby horse is a pony! Hands up everyone who knows what a baby horse is.'

All the right arms in the room, except James's and Miss Smith's, shot upwards. Miss Smith smiled at James.

'Everyone knows,' she said. 'Everyone knows what a baby horse is called except James.'

James thought: I'll run away. I'll join the tinkers and live in a tent.

'What's a baby horse called?' Miss Smith asked the class and the class shouted:

'Foal, Miss Smith.'

'A foal, James,' Miss Smith repeated. 'A baby horse is a foal, James dear.'

'I knew, Miss Smith. I knew, but –'

Miss Smith laughed and the class laughed, and afterwards nobody would play with James because he was so silly to think that a baby horse was a pony.

Activity

We have a certain amount of direct information here in terms of what people said and did (for example, *James became very confused. Miss Smith laughed and the class laughed...*). But what makes the story interesting is how much we work out without being directly told.

1   Use the questions below to interrogate the text. In the process you will see how much detail lies unspoken beneath the surface, in what is sometimes called the subtext:
   •   How can we tell that Miss Smith is a teacher? (We are not told directly.)
   •   How can we tell that she is being cruel?
   •   What do we learn about James Machen?
   •   What impression of the classroom ethos does the writer create?
2   Now compare your response with those given below.

How can we tell that Miss Smith is a teacher?
   •   the way she is addressed as Miss Smith is the first hint
   •   the way she asks questions – outside a classroom someone would be unlikely to ask what a baby horse is called
   •   the fact that she calls James James Machen all the time – naming pupils by their full name

How can we tell that she is being cruel?
This is an interesting example. The surface level of the text says *Miss Smith smiled at James*. An uncertain reader might take this as affection or kindness. But look at the hints of her cruel treatment:
   •   She says publicly to the class *Well, well, James Machen doesn't know what a baby horse is called.* The *Well, well* suggests relish or enjoyment of the situation.
   •   She repeats his mistake in calling it a *pony* – again, humiliating him.
   •   She emphasizes that everyone – apart from James – knows the answer.
   •   When he tries to explain that he does know the answer, she laughs – with the class.
In other words, we have here a portrait of fairly vindictive teaching behaviour. And yet no direct description of this cruelty is ever used.

What do we learn about James Machen?
   •   On a surface level, we learn his full name, that he is a young boy in a classroom, and that he cannot remember the answer to a simple question.
   •   From the subtext we realize that he knows the answer but is overpowered by the teacher's public humiliation of him; that he suffers the cruelty badly and quickly contemplates running away; that he feels isolated.

What impression of the classroom ethos does the writer create?
The writer says very little directly about what the classroom ethos (atmosphere) is like. He does not, for example, write: *It was tense.* But there are clues:
   •   The classroom ethos is strict, with Miss Smith dominating. Her control

is evident by the way she asks all the questions and achieves a response from *all the right arms in the room*.

- Miss Smith dominates the behaviour of the group. William Trevor writes: *Miss Smith laughed and the class laughed*. This shows her capacity to shape their behaviour. The fact that afterwards nobody would play with James because he was *so silly* is a sign that her judgement of James has become their judgement.

- The classroom is a place of humiliation. Although there is laughter, it is controlled by the teacher and used to put a young boy in his place. The ethos of the classroom is a sadistic and menacing one.

Assignment

Read the opening of the short story, *The Other Woman*, by Doris Lessing and use the questions below to develop further your ability to read beneath the surface of text:

- What do you think the writer means when she describes the young policeman as *awkward with sympathy* (line 3)?
- What clues are there that Rose's inner feelings are different from the composed exterior she displays?
- How can you tell that Rose is fighting to keep control of herself?
- Do you think we are expected to like the character of Rose? Why or why not?
- What clues might the title of the story give about Rose's feelings?

···

The Other Woman

Rose's mother was killed one morning crossing the street to do her shopping. Rose was fetched from work, and a young policeman, awkward with sympathy, asked questions and finally said; 'You ought to tell your Dad, miss, he ought to know.' It had struck him as strange that she had not suggested it, but behaved as if the responsibility for everything must of course be hers. He thought Rose was too composed to be natural. Her mouth was set and there was a strained look in her eyes. He insisted; Rose sent a message to her father; but when he came she put him straight to bed with a cup of tea. Mr Johnson was a plump, fair little man, with wisps of light hair lying over a rosy scalp, and blue, candid, trustful eyes. Then she came back to the kitchen and her manner told the policeman that she expected him to leave. From the door he said diffidently; 'Well, I'm sorry, miss, I'm really sorry. A terrible thing – you can't rightly blame the lorry-driver, and your mum – it wasn't her fault, either.' Rose turned her white, shaken face, her cold and glittering eyes towards him and said tartly: 'Being sorry doesn't mend broken bones.' That last phrase seemed to take her by surprise, for she winced, her face worked in a rush of tears, and then she clenched

5

10

15

her jaw again. 'Them lorries' she said heavily, 'them machines, they ought to be stopped, that's what I think.' This irrational remark encouraged the policeman: it was nearer to the tears, the emotion that he thought would be good for her. He remarked encouragingly: 'I daresay, miss, but we couldn't do without them, could we now?' Rose's face did not change. She said politely 'Yes?' It was sceptical and dismissing; that monosyllable said finally: 'You keep your opinions, I'll keep mine.' It examined and dismissed the whole machine age. The young policeman, still lingering over his duty, suggested: 'Isn't there anybody to come and sit with you? You don't look too good, miss, and that's a fact.' 20 25 30

'There isn't anybody,' said Rose briefly, and added: 'I'm all right.' She sounded irritated, and so he left. She sat down at the table and was shocked at herself for what she had said. She thought: I ought to tell George… But she did not move. She stared vaguely around the kitchen, her mind dimly churning around several ideas. One was that her father had taken it hard, she would have her hands full with him. Another, that policemen, officials – they were all nosy parkers, knowing what was best for everybody. She found herself staring at a certain picture on the wall, and thinking: 'Now I can take that picture down. Now she's gone I can do what I like.' She felt a little guilty, but almost at once she briskly rose and took the picture down. It was of a battleship in a stormy sea, and she hated it. She put it away in a cupboard. Then the white empty square on the wall troubled her, and she replaced it by a calendar with yellow roses on it. Then she made herself a cup of tea and began cooking her father's supper, thinking; I'll wake him up and make him eat, do him good to have a bite of something hot. 35 40 45

....

Exploring Genres

This section will develop your response to two very different genres: crime fiction and journalism.

Crime Fiction

This section explores the way that crime fiction writers use written style to achieve their effects.

In the 1920s and 1930s detective fiction was by far the most popular genre. As the German playwright Bertolt Brecht said: 'The crime novel, like the world itself, is ruled by the English'. The most famous lines ever written in crime fiction came from a novel of this period called *Malice Aforethought*:

It was not until several weeks after he had decided to murder his wife that Dr Bickleigh took any active steps in the matter. Murder is a serious business.

Early crime novels were whodunits, the crime had already been committed and it was up to the hero-detective to follow the clues to the murderer.

Later in the century readers have become more interested in the crime itself. Writers like Patricia Cornwall show the gory reality of murder and trace the work of forensic scientists as they piece together scientific evidence to find the suspect.

Here are the openings to two crime stories, one written in the nineteenth century, one written in the twentieth century. As you read them, look for the similarities and differences in the way each writer draws the reader in.

....

A   The Shooting Party

About seven o'clock in the morning the village elder and his assistants whom I had sent for, arrived. It was impossible to drive to the scene of the crime: the rain that had begun in the night was still pouring down in buckets. Little puddles had become lakes. The grey sky looked gloomy, and there was no promise of sunlight. The soaked trees appeared dejected with their dropping branches, and sprinkled a whole shower of large drops at every gust of wind. It was impossible to go there. Besides, it might have been useless. The trace of the crime, such as bloodstains, human footprints, etc., had probably been washed away during the night. But the formalities demanded that the scene of the crime should be examined, and I deferred this visit until the arrival of the police, and in the meantime I made out a draft of the official report of the case, and occupied myself with the examination of witnesses. First of all I examined the gypsies. The poor singers had passed the whole night sitting up in the ballrooms expecting horses to be sent round to convey them to the station. But horses were not provided; the servants, when asked, only sent them to the devil, warning them at the same time that his Excellency had forbidden anybody to be admitted to him. They were also not given the samovar they asked for in the morning. The perplexing and ambiguous situation in which they found themselves in a strange house in which a corpse was lying, the uncertainty as to when they could get away, and the damp melancholy weather had driven the gypsies, both men and women, into such a state of distress that in one night they had become thin and pale. They wandered about from room to room, evidently much alarmed and expecting some serious issue. By my examination I only increased their anxiety. First because my lengthy examination delayed their departure from the accursed house indefinitely, and secondly because it alarmed them. The simple people, imagining that they were seriously suspected of the murder, began to assure me with tears in their eyes, that were not guilty and knew nothing about the matter. Tina, seeing me as an official personage, quite forgot our former connection, and while speaking to me trembled and almost fainted with fright like a little girl about to be whipped. In reply to my request not to be excited, and my assurance that I saw in them nothing but witnesses, the assistants of justice, they informed me in one voice that they had never been witnesses, they knew nothing, and that they trusted in future God would deliver them from all close acquaintance with ministers of the law.

Anton Chekhov

B   The Killers

The door of Henry's lunch-room opened and two men came in. They sat down at the counter.

'What's yours?' George asked them.

'I don't know,' one of the men said, 'What do you want to eat, Al?'

'I don't know,' said Al. 'I don't know what I want to eat.'

Outside it was getting dark. The street-light came on outside the window. The two men at the counter read the menu. From the other end of the counter Nick Adams watched them. He had been talking to George when they came in.

'I'll have a roast pork tenderloin with apple sauce and mashed potatoes,' the first man said.

'It isn't ready yet.'

'What the hell do you put it on the card for?'

'That's the dinner,' George explained. 'You can get that at six o'clock.'

George looked at the clock on the wall behind the counter.

'It's five o'clock.'

'The clock says twenty minutes past five,' the second man said.

'It's twenty minutes fast.'

'Oh, to hell with the clock,' the first man said. 'What have you got to eat?'

'I can give you any kind of sandwiches,' George said. 'You can have ham and eggs, bacon and eggs, or a steak.'

'Give me the chicken croquettes with green peas and cream sauce and mashed potatoes.'

'That's the dinner.'

'Everything we want's the dinner, eh? That's the way you work it.'

'I can give you ham and eggs, bacon and eggs, liver-'

'I'll take the ham and eggs,' the man called Al said. He wore a derby hat and a black overcoat buttoned across the chest. His face was small and white and he had tight lips. He wore a silk muffler and gloves.

'Give me bacon and eggs,' said the other man. He was about the same size as Al. Their faces were different, but they were dressed like twins. Both wore overcoats too tight for them. They sat leaning forward, their elbows on the counter.

Ernest Hemmingway

....

Activity

1   Compare the way the two writers create a feeling of atmosphere:
* What do we learn of the settings?
* How much detail is given?

2   Text A uses a more descriptive style; Text B uses dialogue. What effect does each style have in:
* helping us to know who the characters are
* moving the story along
* making us want to keep reading?

3   Pick out some examples to show the complexity of the vocabulary and sentence structure in Text A that mark it out as the nineteenth-century text, and evidence from Text B that it is more modern.

Journalism

Journalism has been described as 'writing in a hurry', and we usually think of it as reporting the news. In fact there are other styles of journalism too – such as the feature article (something not usually linked directly to a news story), an editorial (giving an opinion about a news story), or a writer's column (in which readers expect to be entertained by a writer's view of life).

   This unit asks you to compare and contrast two news stories: one from a tabloid, the other from a broadsheet newspaper.

Tabloid Format

Here is the report in a tabloid newspaper of a freak tornado in the town of Selsey. The margin notes highlight the main features of tabloid format and style.

Key terms

Tabloid: small format, mass circulation newspaper, such as the *Sun,* the *Mirror,* the *Daily Express,* the *Daily Mail.*

Broadsheet: large format paper, sometimes called the 'quality press', usually aimed at a more educated audience – for example, *The Times,* the *Guardian,* the *Independent,* the *Daily Telegraph.*

I peeped out from sheets ... the wall had gone and I was staring at the sea

by NICK PARKER

A dad banished to a spare bedroom for snoring woke to find the Selsey tornado had ripped away the entire outer wall.

Terrified Jeremy Wearn, 36, peeped above his bedclothes as the winds died away and found himself staring out to SEA.

The Xerox engineer said yesterday: "The wall had just been torn off the side of our house. The end of the bed was only four feet away from where the wall used to be. I just stared in disbelief."

Jeremy, an allergy sufferer, had been packed off to the spare room by wife Donna, 33, because she was fed up with his snoring.

headline to catch the reader's attention

topic sentence tells the story in brief – who, where and what

subject is called by his first name – makes us feel sympathetic towards him

main subject of story is labelled by age and job

plenty of active verbs to keep the story lively

short paragraphs to keep the story moving quickly

plenty of active verbs to keep the story lively

brief quotation to show what the subject's view of what happened

dramatic, easy-to-understand vocabulary – makes the story exciting and straightforward

The *Sun*, 9 January 1998

Activity

Try writing in a similar style. Imagine the tornado puts a garage roof through a pensioner's bedroom window. Use these details to construct the story, using a headline and around 150 words of text:

- Pensioner: Joan McGilvray
- age: 66
- The roof was picked up from 50ft away, from the garden of Ron Burchell.

Make your story as lively and entertaining as possible. Then turn to page 19 to look at how it was actually written up in the *Sun*.

Broadsheet Format

Activity

Now compare the presentation of a news story in a broadsheet newspaper.

How would you expect it to differ in its written style?

Read the story on page 18 and then use the checklist on page 19 to interrogate its style.

Kraken or tree trunk? Mystery blob from the deep confounds the experts

Is it a dead dinosaur? A rotting shark? The last remains of Mr Blobby? One thing's for sure – it's big, smelly and on a Tasmanian beach. Beyond that, says *Charles Arthur,* **Science Editor, nobody seems to want to commit themselves.**

Is it animal, vegetable, or mineral? We can at least say that it's not mineral. But for the moment, it is very hard to be any more specific about this huge mass of matter that washed up on Four Mile Beach in Tasmania earlier this week.

If you do happen to have lost a twenty-foot, four tonne, fishy-smelling, fibre-covered object apparently sporting at least six tentacly legs (or leggy tentacles) recently, maybe you could get in touch with the coastguard there. In the meantime, scientists are puzzling over what this... Blob could be. In the past, decaying objects that have fetched up on beaches have been identified as rotting whale blubber, which does dehydrate to form leather fibres like those visible in the photograph. However, you don't usually get 'legs' or 'tentacles' in blubber.

Marine biologists are used to getting asked about strange beached objects. 'There is certainly a recurrence of things about 15 to 20 feet long being washed up,' said Oliver Crimmen of the Natural History Museum yesterday.

Certainly. Reports have come from as far apart as Scotland, Russia, New Zealand and South Africa, and positive identification (if you can be positive of something so formless) at least back to the 1920s.

'They generally turn out to be rotting basking sharks,' explained Mr Crimmon.

Aha! So could the Blob be an ex-shark? 'They can grow up to 34 feet, and rot down to something like a sea monster,' said Mr Crimmen. 'Of course, whales can too... and elephant seals... and squids...'

Yes, but what about this one? 'Hmm. Well, judging from the photos, and what they show of the 'legs' and 'hair' – well, they don't add up to the decomposition of any known organism. We haven't ascertained yet even whether it's an animal. The fact that it is reported to smell fishy doesn't mean much – any marine thing with sediment and weed is going to smell. What we really need is some clue about what's inside.'

Scientists in Tasmania are reported to be planning DNA tests on their mysterious lump. Mr Crimmen reckons though that this is 'rather like doing a DNA test on a corpse before you've checked its

pockets'. He suggested that the first step is to look for any bones or other skeletal tissue. Although from its appearance he reckons it has been rotting in the water for 'several weeks', even the cartilage of a basking shark will survive, especially the spine – and the picture does seem to show a spine curving away (at the top right).

The most exciting possibility would be if this is the carcass of a plesiosaur, a dinosaur which had a long neck and paddle-like limbs. But to be sure, someone has to poke it with a stick and find some bones. The best efforts in Tasmania haven't turned any up yet.

And in the end it might all turn out not to be an animal at all. 'That fibrous matter could mean... well, we can't rule out that it's not the bole of a mangrove tree,' said Mr Crimmen. 'But when I showed it to a botanist he didn't recognize it.' Clearly, he's in good company.

The *Independent*, 10 January 1998

Roof landed in bedroom

PENSIONER Joan McGilvray was dozing off when a garage roof crashed through her bedroom window.

It was torn off a building 50ft away and hurled at her home 'like a frisbee,' Joan, 66, said: 'There was an almighty crash and the window just seemed to explode.

'Dozens of heavy roof tiles flew in at the same time and I'm amazed I wasn't hurt. It was terrifying. I was left cowering until it passed.

'I can't believe such a huge roof could have flown so far.'

Neighbour Ron Burchell said the felt covered wooden roof was ripped off his garage in one piece.

His conservatory windows were also blown in and his car port reduced to matchwood.

Ron, 7- - in bed with wife Iris, 67, when the tornado struck - said: 'I first realized it was serious when the hailstones began battering the house. The noise became deafening.'

The *Sun*, 9 January 1998

Checklist style	questions
Headline	How does it attempt to grab the reader's interest? Does the language level seem higher than in the tabloid? How can you tell?
Writer's Attitude	Is it serious, humorous, aiming to entertain rather than inform? How can you tell?
Opening Paragraph	How does the writer use language here? Why use the opening questions? How easy-to-follow is the language? Does the paragraph make you want to read on?
Labelling of People	How are people labelled? Is the technique different from in the tabloid paper?
Accessibility	How easy to follow overall is the story? How complex are the sentences? How accessible is the vocabulary? Did you encounter many words which are unfamiliar?

Assignment

This unit has shown you a variety of the higher order reading skills that you will need to achieve top grades in English at GCSE. Using the grid below, undertake your own audit of the skills you have already and those that need further development.

Reading Skill	Strength – where am I already using this?	Weakness – what do I need to do to develop this?
Analysing written texts: scanning skimming key words summarizing		
Reading beneath the surface of texts		
Identifying the language features of genres		

2

Original Writing

spotless, tiled bathroom, transfixed by the thin strip of pink paper in her hand. Downstairs, the door slammed shut; the noise echoing around her head but not registering. The vibrations of his footsteps on each stair shuddered steadily through her. His voice called her name excitedly, yet growing curious as he received no encouraging response. A mounting number of doors were opened and briefly glanced into, his eyes sweeping round each room with then closed again when they produced nothing. The curiosity was turning into worry; tenderness suddenly sharply

An A* candidate is expected to write with flair and originality. Such writing would be exciting to read as well as challenging. Paragraphs and sentences would be fluently connected and varied in length. The piece would feel alive and it would be obvious that the writer had a clear sense of purpose and audience in mind.

Study Skills

This unit will focus on what makes a good short story and how to write one. Skills you will work on include:

- How to start writing your own stories
- Openings and endings
- Rewriting existing stories

Getting Started

You need to understand the importance of planning and the different types that you can use. For example:

- **Brainstorming:** writing down as many different ideas as possible, not necessarily in any specific order. Your page should end up looking quite chaotic but it's a good way of avoiding the writer's block that a plain sheet of A4 can produce and also of kick-starting your imagination.

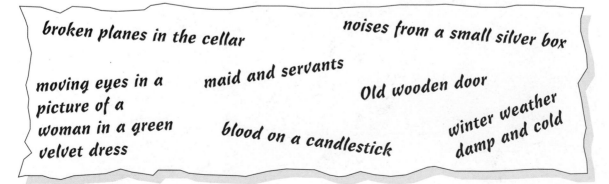

broken planes in the cellar

noises from a small silver box

moving eyes in a picture of a woman in a green velvet dress

maid and servants

Old wooden door

blood on a candlestick

winter weather damp and cold

- **Spider Diagram:** the body of a spider forms your main idea and the legs, thoughts or avenues that relate to this that can be explored in the story. This encourages you to see each idea as part of a connected series.

Island looks like a house

House takes on appearance of a hospital

JOURNEY

She's in hospital with a drip in her arm

begin to dream – escape to an island

Could link Hospital to REALITY (island is DREAM of journey)

- **Question Diagram:** similar to the spider diagram but the purpose of this is asking and then answering specific questions. Start in the middle with an idea then pursue it and stretch it with questions and answers.

BLACK MARSH

What? strong smells of damp leaves and rain

How does it appear? Small at first then grows to expanse

Where? Middle of a forest

- **Paragraph Plan:** this is when you have a clear idea what your story will be about. Aim to plan five paragraphs with four bullet points for each. Give each paragraph a subheading and briefly list beneath the things that will happen or key features. For example:

Paragraph 1 – Journey to Germany
- Scenery closing in, feeling claustrophobic
- Memories of last visit – pale faces
- Back to reality – description of carriage (contrast)
- Arrival – slow, smell of smoke mingled with a winter evening

Activity

1 From the following list, brainstorm two stories separately. Give yourself 60 seconds on each one and try to write down as many different ideas that occur to you as possible:

- The cellar
- Burnt remains of a car
- A dripping wet wooden trunk
- Man running fast down the street carrying a suitcase
- A chess game

This is difficult when you first start; our imagination can become rusty through lack of use. You will find though that ideas emerge which may surprise you. The trick is not to be too lateral in your thinking – be different. Hopefully, one of the two chaotic pages will have the makings of a good story.

Openings and endings

Read the openings and endings of these two short stories:

....

A   The Lottery

The first that Ted Bilborough knew of his wife's good fortune was when one of his friends, an elderly wag, shook his hand with mock gravity and murmured a few words of manly but inappropriate sympathy. Ted didn't know what to make of it. He had just stepped from the stairway onto the upper deck of the 6:15pm ferry from town. Fred Lewis seemed to have been waiting for him, and, as he looked about he got the impression of newspapers and grins and a little flutter of half derisive excitement, all focused on himself. Everything seemed to bulge towards himself. It must be some sort of leg pull. He felt his assurance threatened, and the corner of his mouth twitched uncomfortably in his fat cheek, as he tried to assume a hard boiled manner…

…She came and stood in front of him, her back to the littered table, her total body taut. 'I suppose you're wondering what I am going to do? I'll tell you. I'm going away. By myself. Before it's too late. I'm going tomorrow.'

He didn't seem to be taking it in.

'Beattie will come and look after you and the children. She'll be glad to. It won't cost you a penny more than it does now,' she added.

He stood staring at her, her flaccid hands hanging down, his face sagging.

'Then you meant what you said in the paper. "Last hope?"' he said.

'Yes,' she answered.

Marjorie Barnard

....

B   The Man without a Temperament

'He stood at the hall door turning the ring, turning the heavy signet ring upon his little finger while his glance traveled coolly, deliberately over the round tables and basket chairs scattered around in the glassed-in veranda. He persed his lips – he might have been going to whistle – but he did not whistle – only turned the ring – turned the ring on his pink, freshly washed hands.

Over in the corner sat the two Topknots, drinking a decoction they always drank at this hour – something whitish, greyish, in glasses, with little husks floating on the top – and rooting in a tin full of paper shavings for pieces of speckled biscuit, which they broke, dropped into the glasses and fished for with spoons. Their two coils of knitting, like two snakes, slumbered beside the tray…

…He hears her stirring. Does she want something?

'Boggles?'

Good lord! She is talking in her sleep. They haven't used that name for years.

'Boggles. Are you awake?'

'Yes, do you want something?'

'Oh, I'm going to be a bother. I'm so sorry. Do you mind? There's a wretched mosquito inside my net – I can hear him singing. Would you catch him? I don't want to move because of my heart.'

'No, don't move. Stay where you are.' He switches on the light, lifts the net.

'Where is the little beggar? Have you spotted him?'

'Yes, there, over by the corner. Oh, I do feel such a fiend to have dragged you out of bed. Do you mind dreadfully?'

'No, of course not.' For a moment he hovers in his blue and white pyjamas. Then, 'got him,' he said.

'Oh good. Was he a juicy one?'

'Beastly.' He went over to the washstand

and dipped his fingers in water. 'Are you all right now? Shall I switch off the light?'

'Yes, please. No Boggles! Come back here a moment. Sit down by me. Give me your hand.' She turns his signet ring. 'Why weren't you asleep? Boggles, listen. Come closer. I sometimes wonder – do you mind awfully being out here with me?'

He bends down. He kisses her. He tucks her in, he smooths the pillow.

'Rot!' he whispers.

Katherine Mansfield

. . . .

Activity

1 Think about what you learn from the opening and ending of both of these stories. In the beginning of the first we are given the name of Ted Bilborough but in the second, the man is referred to as *he* until much later on.
- What do you think the significance of this is?
- Look at the note of finality with which both of these stories end. How can we recognize an ending?

2 In pairs discuss what you think happened in the middle of these stories and then choose one to write up using the same beginning and ending provided but with your middle link between the two. Bear in mind the criteria for good writing outlined at the beginning of this unit.

3 In pairs write down the following:
- The name of a fictional person
- A characteristic of that person
- A place
- A sentence of speech

Next, swap your list with your partner. You now have fifteen minutes to write a story that includes and links all four items in a believable way.

What Makes a Good Story?

David Almond is a short story writer and a novelist. You can read one of his short stories on page 78. Below are a few of his statements about short stories:

Short stories move quickly. Every word works. Nothing is flabby or loose. The language is specific rather than general, concrete rather than abstract. Short stories do not refer to a world: they present a world and make us experience that world. They show us things, rather than telling us about things. Short stories are not neat little assemblies of beginnings, middles and ends. Short stories often move cinematically, taking us abruptly from scene to scene. Short stories focus closely on their subjects, but they imply and suggest a whole world of experience. Short stories are broad, not narrow, in their effect. The plot can be minuscule.

The short story does not deal in earth shattering events, except in showing how those events affect intimate human lives. The short story writer understands the things that really keep us awake at night: global warming, the nuclear threat, poverty per-haps. But more powerfully: a nagging memory, the crack in the bedroom ceiling, the ten-pound note that we lost, the way that girl/boy turned away from our smile. The short story is intimate. Short stories do not depend on twists in the tail, cop-out endings. The end might be left hanging.

There is not a predetermined short story form. Every story is an experience that draws the reader quickly into its world. Stories are about secrets, lies, hidden things that might be exposed, disguises, little searches and excavations. They are about journeys, quests, discoveries. Short stories work on our senses. We taste, hear, smell, see, touch the story's fictional world. Short stories are strong on naming: they do not say flower, they say what kind of flower. Short stories do not trade in loose adjectives or empty adverbs. They depend on the stronger effects of nouns and verbs. Stories are living things, elemental things, among the most important things in the world. In a short story, we can hear the echoes of fairy tales, myths, legends, jokes, the Bible, the Arabian Nights, the sto-ries told to us by grandmothers, toddlers, mad uncles, the stories chanted around fires in Ice Age caves.

Make a list of the main points David Almond is making then look again at the two short stories on pages 22–24. Using your list analyse the ways in which the stories either exemplify his points or seem to contradict them.

Activity

Read this section of Fay Weldon's short story entitled *The Weekend* and think about David Almond's points again. What techniques are being used here? Consider:

- Detail
- Language
- Theme
- Structure
- Imagination

The Weekend

By seven-thirty they were ready to go. Martha had everything packed into the car and the three children appropriately dressed and in the back seat, complete with educational games and wholewheat biscuits. When everything was ready in the car Martin would switch off the television, come downstairs, lock up the house, front and back, and take the wheel.

Weekend! Only two hours' drive down to the cottage on Friday evenings, three hours' drive back on Sunday nights. The pleasures of greenery and guests in between. They reckoned themselves fortunate, how fortunate!

On Fridays Martha would get home on the bus at six-twelve and prepare tea and sandwiches for the family: then she would strip four beds and put the sheets and quilt covers in the washing machine for Monday: take the country bedding from the airing basket, plus the books and games, plus the weekend food – acquired at intervals throughout the week, to lessen the load – plus her own folder of work from the office, plus Martin's drawing materials (she was a market researcher in an advertising agency, he a freelance designer) plus hairbrushes, jeans, spare T-shirts, Jolyon's antibiotics (he suffered from sore throats), Jenny's recorder, Jasper's cassette player and so on – ah, the so on! – and would pack them all, skillfully and quickly, into the boot. Very little could be left in the cottage during the week. ('An open invitation to burglars': Martin.) Then Martha would run round the house tidying and wiping, doing this and that, finding the cat at one neighbour's and delivering it to another, while the others ate their tea; and would usually, proudly, have everything finished by the time they had eaten their fill. Martin would just catch the BBC2 news, while Martha cleared away the tea table, and the children tossed up for the best positions in the car. 'Martha,' said Martin, tonight, 'you ought to get Mrs Hodder to do more. She takes advantage of you.'

Mrs Hodder came in twice a week to clean. She was over seventy. She charged two pounds an hour. Martha paid her out of her own wages: well, the running of the house was Martha's concern. If Martha chose to go out to work – as was her perfect right, Martin allowed, even though it wasn't the best thing for the children, but that must be Martha's moral responsibility – Martha must surely pay her domestic stand-in. An evident truth, heard loud and clear and frequent in Martin's mouth and Martha's heart.

'I expect you're right,' said Martha. She did not want to argue. Martin had had a long hard week, and now had to drive. Martha couldn't. Martha's licence had been suspended four months back for drunken driving. Everyone agreed that the suspension was unfair: Martha seldom drank to excess: she was for one thing usually too busy pouring drinks for other people or washing other people's glasses to get much inside herself. But Martin had taken her out to dinner on her birthday, as was his custom, and exhaustion and excitement mixed had made her imprudent, and before she knew where she was, why there she was, in the dock, with a distorted lamp-post to pay for and a new bonnet for the car and six months' suspension.

So now Martin had to drive her car down to the cottage, and he was always tired on Fridays, and hot and sleepy on Sundays and every rattle and clank and bump in the engine she felt to be somehow her fault.

Martin had a little sports car for London and work: it could nip in and out of the traffic nicely: Martha's was an old estate car, with room for the children, picnic baskets, bedding, food, games, plants, drink, portable television and all the things required by the middle classes for weekends in the country. It lumbered rather than zipped and made Martin angry. He seldom spoke a harsh word, but Martha, after the fashion of wives, could detect his mood from what he did not say rather than what he did, and from the tilt of his head, and the way his crinkly, merry eyes seemed crinklier and merrier still – and of course from the way he addressed Martha's car.

'Come along, you old banger you! Can't you do better than that?'

· ·

Activity

Despite the fact that this is not written as a first person narrative we feel as though it could almost be an extract from Martha's diary. The structure of this piece is unusual:

- some paragraphs are very short whilst others feel overburdened
- commas are used to separate items in the form of a list nearly all the way through
- comments made by Martin are in brackets
- the names of Martin and Martha are repeated in nearly every line
- there is a lack of full stops

When we add all of these together, what do you think Fay Weldon intends? What is it that she is trying to achieve? Think about how cleverly the character of Martin is created without featuring as directly as Martha.

Using some of the techniques mentioned above and any that you can add to the list, write a continuation of this piece that is to be no more than one side of A4. Imagine that Jasper has had an accident at their cottage in front of their guests. Martha must take him to hospital but she is also needed to prepare their lunch. ('*Guests must never be kept waiting*': Martin.)

Rewriting Tales

Angela Carter's *Company of Wolves* is a gothic version of *Red Riding Hood*. Read this extract.

• •

Company of Wolves

'One beast and only one howls in the woods by night. The wolf is carnivore incarnate and he's as cunning as he is ferocious; once he's had a taste of flesh then nothing else will do. At night, the eyes of the wolves shine like candle flames, yellowish, reddish, but that is because the pupils of their eyes fatten on the darkness and catch the light from your lantern to flash it back to you – red for danger; if a wolf's eyes reflect only the moonlight, then they gleam a cold and unnatural green, a mineral, a piercing colour. If the benighted traveler spies those luminous, terrible sequins stitched suddenly on the black thickets, then he knows he must run, if fear has not struck him stock-still.'

• •

See how menacing this has become. This section is the beginning of the story but you can see already that it has the feel of a legend that is passed down from one generation to the next, possibly sitting round a fire in the darkness of night.

Activity

Take a well-known tale such as *Snow White, Red Riding Hood, Cinderella* and turn it into something malevolent. Perhaps Snow White is not all she seems. She might be cruel and cold but seem pure. Below is an example of what can be achieved:

• •

One squirrel, however, ran across her path and stopped, transfixed, mesmerized by her pale gaze. Gently she stooped, picked up the squirrel and began to stroke it from the top of its head to the tip of its tail, its tiny heart trembling rapidly under her caress. Then she grasped its neck between her long fingers and snapped it in two. Tossing the limp body aside she continued on her way, leaving the tiny patch of fur to be swallowed up by darkness on the stony forest floor.

Soon she came to a small cottage in a quiet clearing in the heart of the forest. Steeped in moonlight, a smouldering blanket of silence weighed down so heavily that it stifled the sound of her slight footsteps, the silver light reflecting in the mirror-like discs in her face. The moon glowed distantly, shrouded in black. She entered the cottage through a door which led straight into a warm, welcoming kitchen with a roaring fire in the hearth. As she stepped forward, emanating a cool serenity, seven pairs of eyes swivelled round to meet her steady gaze.

'My name is Snow White,' she said. 'I have lost my way in this dark forest and I have no bed to sleep in. Please help me.'

The seven dwarves who sat round the table found their hearts were melted by Snow White's youthful beauty. One of them said:

'We cannot do anything but help you, my child. Please stay with me and my brothers for as long as you please.' The others nodded their heads in agreement, and so it was settled. Snow White joined the dwarves and each day they brought her gifts of bluebells, primroses and stray animals they had found and laid them before her feet. The flowers, however, withered under her gaze and the animals disappeared without trace. The sky darkened as her beauty grew more each day, becoming stronger as she flourished in the clear forest air.

· ·

Activity

For each of the following words allow yourself one minute to write down as many ideas that you associate with it as possible:

- black
- tunnel
- salt
- lice
- satin

You should have impressive collections of ideas. Choose the one that you feel has most potential and read it through again. Look to see if you can use each of the following in your list:

- alliteration
- simile/metaphor
- appeal to senses
- descriptive detail

Now, write a short story based on the word you chose. Think about the language you use to make this a stylized and stylish piece that appeals to the senses and shows flair and originality in language use. For example:
In balmy breath blackness she blundered; searching for light…

Assignments

1 Look at the following scenario:

> A man is seen leaving a house with a large crocodile skin bag under his arm. He has pitted skin and is obviously sweating. He leaves the door open wide enough for a cat to sneak in and doesn't look back. His footsteps are uneven and one foot sounds heavier than the other. One hour later another man leaves the same property. He shuts the door carefully and, pulling down his hat, begins to whistle.

Bearing in mind what you have learnt about the ingredients of a good short story, write three different perspectives on the scenario above. Each is to be one side of A4 in length and in a different style. The three perspectives are:

- From the perspective of the first man leaving
- From the perspective of the cat
- From the perspective of the cleaning lady who visits for an hour every Tuesday morning

Aim for originality in your approach and make the reader think. You might, for example, want the cat to sound educated so you would use a formal and slightly superior tone.

2 Take the theme of loneliness. Write down everything that you associate with it. Try to be broad in your thought and not just think about homeless or old people. Think of all the different ways in which a person can be lonely. Write a story in which you follow one of these people and comment on their actions, behaviour and the way they seem to be living. You are never spotted and are not known to the person so may not speak to them. Try and be sensitive in the way you describe their body language as well as the speech you overhear. Your aim is to create a touching portrayal of loneliness.

3 Select a story or write one yourself to tell to an audience. Read it through and decide whether to edit it and write notes by the side indicating when there is a climax in the story, when to raise your voice and when to lower it. You need to have read this through enough times so that you almost know it off by heart. This will help in your telling of the story because eye contact helps to ensure that the attention of your audience does not waver.

4 The title of your story is simply *Echo*. Brainstorm what this means to you first. Now, answer the following questions:
- What colour is your echo?
- What makes it special?

- What noise does it make?
- Does it exist in the past, present or future?
- What does it signify?

Now, think about telling the story of this echo. You can use the following as inspiration. The two extracts below have been written by GCSE students and demonstrate what can be achieved.

A They invaded my mind like savages and took what they could – my sanity. It happens all too often. But now it doesn't seem the same – now it happens differently. Sometimes, there is no warning and sometimes there is. Footsteps. Just walking along, with no direction. I can hear them. They're coming straight for me. They arrive; the bustling of autumn trees as the wind passes through them, autumn leaves being crunched under foot. That's what I hear. That's how I know they've arrived; voices in an unmelodic chorus.

'Please help… we need you… help… I am… It's too fast… slow it down… it's going to kill me!' Wham! Nothing. Again, I am alone. My life returns to a state of temporary normality but I know it won't ever be the same again.

Out on the Moors, the night engulfed the plains. It was like my mind; it wasn't my own anymore, it belonged to someone else. I was dying and I knew it. But I am still here today. Henry does still visit me. I still fear him. I don't know why. I should be used to it all by now but I'm not. I never will be. Nobody ever could.

I'm not special. There's nothing special about what happens to me. What happens to me hurts. It hurts and causes me pain. I am not alone. Never will I be. Never can I be, not so long as I have the echo.

By Robert Hudson 11E

B A spoken word is greeted with a barricade of defence, questioned and queried, in which time the point is lost and the echo is provoked once more. Another recurrence of a spoken image conveyed into a mind which has been eroded to the extent that the notion is projected into only a framework of scaffolding – contained within it, only emptiness. The hallucination of imagination has been erased so that opinions have drained and we are becoming controlled. Through time, the echo has grown louder as it now vibrates through a skull rather than a mind and the voice is mechanical and adapted to a creation of solitary correctness. Dragged down to a level beyond hierarchy, a human is reduced to insignificance. What is said is often irrelevant, how it is received is the problem.

By Suzy Kay 11C

3

Media 1 Advertising

The first washing machine with a unique Stain-Action programme

But HURRY – for a limited time only!

BRITAIN'S
BEST-SELLING
MAGAZINE

A great deal now... a great deal more later

An A* candidate will be able to comment upon the way in which language is used to persuade. They would be expected to consider the layout as well as the structure, and analyse the success of the text, relating this to the purpose and audience.

Study Skills

This unit will develop your ability to analyse and write about different types of advertisements. Looking at the text in the light of the four areas below will help to inform your initial impression:

- **Considering the Purpose** – apart from hoping to persuade us, does the text aim to do anything else? Is it trying to make us feel guilty so we'll be persuaded to give more money to charity? Are we being praised?

- **Deciding on the Appropriate Audience** – who is the text aimed at? Teenagers? Fashion conscious people in their early twenties? Retired people who want to make the most of their leisure time?

- **Analysing the Structure** – how is the text laid out? Look at the presentation: pictures, diagrams, headings and subheadings, paragraph and sentence length.

- **Commenting upon the Tone** – consider how it sounds. The key to this is the use of language. If the language is formal then the tone is likely to be also. Similarly, if the language is colloquial then it is likely that the tone will have an informal and friendly feel.

Techniques of Persuasion

There are five techniques of persuasion. You need to be familiar with these in order to complete this unit.

1   **Assertion** – this is where a point of view is expressed as though it is a universally accepted fact. For example:

    'Our dog food <u>is</u> the best on the market today'

This works well because we associate facts with informative writing where there is no bias. Therefore, we believe that what we are being told is the truth, has evidence to substantiate it and is believed to be correct by many people. This is the most common persuasive technique.

2   **Positive selection** – again, this is common in advertising and it is clear why. The advertisers only choose to mention the more positive aspects of their product. It would be difficult to imagine advertising telling the whole truth! For example:

    '<u>Some</u> people enjoyed eating our new chocolate bar while others felt that it was too sweet'

Selection only mentions people who enjoyed the product.

3   **Repetition** – this is where points are repeated (perhaps the name of the product and/or the telephone number) so that the audience will remember them. Try counting how many times car insurance companies repeat their telephone number during a single advertisement. For example:

    'Phone free on 0800 77 66 55...that's freephone 0800 77 66 55... The number again, 0800 77 66 55 – we're waiting to take your call... on 0800 77 66 55'

You might feel like screaming by the end but the chances are you'll remember the number.

4   **Rhetorical questions** – never underestimate the power of these. Teachers use them all the time as they are an extremely useful way of making it clear what the answer has to be. We all associate questions with a search for knowledge. The person asking the question does not know the answer. Rhetorical questions are different; the person asking the question does know the answer. These type of questions are a powerful tool because they make you think that you are being asked an open question, however, there is only one answer you can give – theirs. It is all about control. Look at these as examples:

'Do you want to be a success?'
'Are you like this at home?'
'Do you want to pass your GCSEs?'

In each case the teacher has forced the pupil to take responsibility for the answer. In advertising the advertiser asks a rhetorical question so that you feel you have come up with the answer yourself. Remember though, it is not your answer it is theirs!

'Would you really wash your clothes in anything less?'
'Hard to beat – isn't it?'
'Don't we all deserve the best?'

5   **Pin-pointing the enemy** – there are two ways that this can be achieved. The first is in *directly* naming your competition. The laws in America permit advertisers to name other brands or companies when they are selling their product. In the UK we use brand 'X' which is pin-pointing the enemy *indirectly*. Both of these are effective because they work through a comparison. If an advertiser compares their product to another directly or indirectly and the other product comes off worse then their product appears all the better. In a capitalist society like ours, where there is a lot of competition between manufacturers and companies, this is very important. For example:

'You'll find our computers much more reliable and better value for money than others on the market.'

Activity

Now look at the advertisment on the opposite page to see how it has been annotated for persuasive techniques. Note the use of the techniques described above: positive selection, repetition, pinpointing the enemy, assertion and rhetorical questions. Consider whether or not they have been effectively employed.

"Céad Míle Fáilte"
A wonderful welcome in anyone's language

Assertion
Opinion is presented as fact (No other country...)

Repetition
A land ... a land ... a land

No other country inspires more lasting, long distance affection than Ireland. A land whose scenic splendour stirs every emotion from pure exhilaration to peaceful calm... A land whose people embrace the spirit of friendship with the warmest of welcomes... A land where life is lived that little bit slower.

Positive Selection
scenic splendour... peaceful calm

And how better to experience it than by staying in an authentic Irish cottage? With over 400 holiday cottages, Country Cottages in Ireland offers the widest choice. Whether you pick a fisherman's cottage in County Cork or a country manor house in County Clare, you'll live among locals, become part of the community – who couldn't help but fall in love with Irish life?

Rhetorical questions
Making us actively think about Irish life

Pinpointing the enemy (indirectly)
The advertisement implies that the competitors are inferior (because we have the widest choice)

For the widest choice of Country Cottages in Ireland request our free 1999 brochure today

CALL 0870 585 1166

QUOTING CODE G2030 OR COMPLETE AND POST THE COUPON BELOW TO:
Country Cottages in Ireland, PO Box 18, Earl Shilton, Leicester, LE9 8ZY

Country Cottages in Ireland

Please send me a priority copy of the 1999 Country Cottages in Ireland brochure

Title(Mr./Mrs./Ms./Other) _____ Initial____ Surname_____

Address_____

_____ Postcode _____

Telephone_____ DOB ___/___/_____

G1005

— *Live the Irish Way of Life* —

Activity

1 Working in a group, bring in magazine advertisements that have caught your eye and place them in order of persuasiveness. Make notes for each advertisement under the following headings: **purpose, audience, structure** and **tone** (P.A.S.T.).

2 Again in a group, take the following slogans and write your own advertisement to go with each. Aim to use all of the persuasive techniques in each:

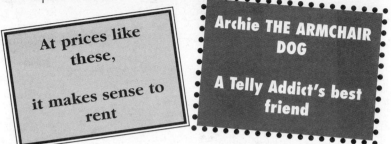

At prices like these,

it makes sense to rent

Archie THE ARMCHAIR DOG

A Telly Addict's best friend

3 Read the following television commercial for cat food. How effective do you think this advertisement is? Annotate the text for persuasive techniques. Is it important as a selling point that the voices of the two cats are Mel Smith and Griff Rhys Jones?

> *Two cats sitting in a laundry basket looking up at washing hanging on a line to dry.*
>
> cat 1: 'Have you ever wondered why humans wear clothes?'
> cat 2: 'I assume it must have something to do with the cold, otherwise they'd be all exposed and hare and –'
> cat 1: 'It actually comes from not getting your Kit-e-Kat mate.'
> cat 2: 'Does it?'
> cat 1: 'Cause Kit-e-Kat gives you your essential fatty acids.'
> cat 2: 'Right. Well they're important are they?'
> cat 1: 'Well they're essential for a good thick coat of healthy hair. Yes.'
> cat 2: 'And humans don't eat Kit-e-Kat?'
> cat 1: 'Apparently not.'
> cat 2: 'Really?'
> cat 1: 'Mad aren't they? Save a fortune in dry cleaning.'
> narrator: 'New Kit-e-Kat – us cats thrive on it.'

4 Make notes on the techniques used in the text below. Look for assertion, pin-pointing the enemy, and repetition. Circle individual words or punctuation which would prove your point. The advertisement has a challenging topic: trying to interest its audience in double glazing. See how well it works.

Graham Rose, Production Director of
Glevum Windows

5 Glevum Windows also advertise on the radio. The style of their advertisement on the radio is less formal and less concerned with providing information. Radio advertisements are limited by time and, as three or four follow each other, they have the task of making theirs memorable and entertaining. The advertisers have to consider carefully:

- Who their audience is
- What their purpose is besides persuading the audience to buy their product
- How to be original
- How to be successful

Imagine that you have been given the task of writing the script for the Glevum Windows radio advertisement. You have two minutes to fill and you must be exact.

- Read through the advertisement and select the main points that you wish to emphasize
- Decide on your audience
- With this in mind, consider the tone and style of your advert
- Decide how you can best meet the needs of your audience – you need to entertain, persuade and captivate them

When you have finished, time yourself. Read it to a partner and get them to tell you how successful they think it is.

6 Now read this radio advert for an alternative window company. It is read with strong country accents as a song.

Man:	'Well, one man went to buy, went to buy new windows. One man and his wife –'
Wife:	'Dot –'
Man:	'went to buy new windows. He'd seen the local rag, there's hundreds he could choose from but the wisdom of his wife –'
Wife:	'Dot –'
Man:	'meant they'd call for Coldseal.'
Wife:	'When buying no deposit until the job's complete –'
Man:	'Ooh argh!'
Wife:	'I'm not having our hard earned cash suddenly depleated.'
Man:	'That's right!'
Wife:	'I want a life time guarantee, one that I can rely on.'
Man:	'She said.'
Wife:	'I don't want any cowboys that I have to keep an eye on.'
Man:	'That's why we're choosing Coldseal and that'll please the wife 0800 22 11 55'
Wife:	'That's right!'

Write an advertorial for this company that would appear in a broadsheet newspaper. Your aim is to inform and persuade your audience that your windows are the best, the most reliable, selling at the best price – a price you can afford to pay. Both language and tone will be formal. When you have finished, compare the two texts and write a comparison with the following as subheadings:

- Audience
- Purpose
- Structure
- Tone
- Effectiveness

Structuring a Critical Response

Read the advertisement below then look at the activity on page 40.

SUPER TROPHIC NEUROMUSCULAR STIMULATION

A unique system which represents the very latest research into the science of beauty. From the age of around nineteen, the signal from the nerve to the muscle begins to slow down, *CLEO11* speaks to the muscles by mimicking the brain signal of a healthy seventeen year old and re-educates the deep postural muscle to work at the correct speed again, re-toning and firming the critical muscle groups. The *CLEO11* is effectively replicating a brain signal, so it really is a natural therapy. This revolutionary compact battery powered machine uses a range of inter-changeable treatment programmes to condition and tone your Face, Hands, Breasts, Shoulders, Buttocks and even the Pelvic Floor muscles. (Especially recommended after child birth.)

REVOLUTIONARY

Have you ever looked at your array of beauty treatments and wished for an all in one beauty system which can do it all? A system which can condition and tone your face, body and even your pelvic floor muscles. Well, it's here at last, because of demand from our existing cleo users

we're launched the *CLEO11* a unique body toning system which represents the very latest technology in the science of beauty.

Our research and development in advanced pulse technology leaves other manufacturers guessing as to how super T.N.S is so effective. Based on scientific medical findings this revolutionary compact battery powered machine uses a range of interchangeable treatment programmes to lift, tone and condition the muscles. Reduce wrinkles on your Face, soften your Hands, lift your Bustline, tone your Shoulders, flatten your Tummy, tone the shape of your Buttocks and tighten your Pelvic Floor Muscles – all with one machine.

REMEMBER only the *CLEO11* uses SUPER TROPHIC STIMULATION the rest can only dream.

IS IT EASY TO USE?

It couldn't be simpler. The *CLEO111* consists of a control unit, leads, self adhesive pads and a range of easy to insert treatment cards, just choose the treatment for the area of your Face or Body you want to exercise, attach the pads and let *CLEO11* do the rest. *CLEO11* is designed to be used in the privacy and comfort of your own home.

Activity

Write a critical response to the Super Trophic advertisement. In structuring your response, you should write an introduction that focuses on your initial impressions of the text: the layout, audience, purpose, structure and tone. The body of your essay should be organized with a paragraph on each section. You should examine persuasive techniques, sentence structure and tone. In your conclusion, comment on how successful you feel the text is when you consider the purpose. Does it achieve what it sets out to? Is the audience successfully targeted?

Assignment

1   In pairs, choose one of the following topics and produce a persuasive talk:

   • School on a Saturday
   • Boys and girls having to wear shorts at school in the summer
   • Homework Club for one hour after school – compulsory attendance
   • A longer school day

You can either choose to be a member of the Senior Management Team, a school prefect or a school governor. You need to remember that for your talk to be a success, you will need to appear informative rather than persuasive. Use bar charts, quote facts and figures and have quotations from those who support you. The more professional you look, the more notice the audience are going to take of you.

They should also award you a grade at the end to indicate how successful they thought your presentation was. If it is a success why not take it into another class to see if they believe your proposals? It is, after all, a mark of genius if you can make a class believe that going into school on a Saturday is a good idea!

The rest of the class should mark you on your performance. They should have a check-list of what they are looking for. (You can shorten these using letters and/or symbols.) Your table could look like this:

CATEGORY	GOOD	WEAK
Assertion		
Positive Selection		
Repetition		
Pin-pointing the Enemy		
Diagrams		
Evidence		
Body Language		
Eye contact		
Tone		

2 Compare advertisements on the television. Select two different time periods of the day, for example, morning, 4pm, 6pm and 9pm. Think carefully about what products are being advertised here. This is a research topic and so you need to utilize everything you have learnt in this unit. Consider:

- Audience
- Tone
- Language

Are the advertisers successfully targeting their audiences?

3 Create a product of your own (as original as possible please) and then imagine that you are a sales representative for the company that produces it. You are going to an important meeting where you have been asked to sell the product to the group listening. Complete the following:

- Write the script of what you are going to say (concentrate on persuasive techniques)

This should be no more than two sides of A4. As this is a presentation you will also need diagrams, facts, figures, quotations from satisfied customers and expert opinions as well as the product itself or at least a picture of it. When these are completed, go back over the script writing in when you need to use each of these aids. Also, write in pauses for dramatic effect and any body language necessary.

4 Read the following letter and answer the essay question below:

- Analyse the 'International Wine' letter. Your analysis should include comments on persuasive techniques, audience, structure and tone. Conclude by saying how effective you think it is.

International Wine Company Ltd

November 1993

Dear Reader

YOURS FREE, WITH EVERY ORDER! Six beautiful 'Sommelier' crystal glasses, worth £12.99

Six beautifully crafted wine glasses are the ideal way to introduce yourself to the International Wine Company and our superb yet inexpensive wines.

They would normally cost you £12.99 elsewhere – yet they're yours, FREE, when you take advantage of this amazing Special Introductory offer.

As a leading importer of the world's top vintages, we can offer all the wines you'll ever need at the most tremendously competitive prices.

Where else, for instance, can you buy a Chablis from the glorious 1992 vintage at an unbelievably low price of just £4.99 a bottle?

Where else, can you buy Piper-Heidsieck Champagne for only £11.99?

No other wine merchant, we believe, can currently offer you such stupendous value!

So please take a look at all we have to offer.

And then consider all these additional benefits:

- Outstanding wine offers, together with colour brochures, to study in the comfort of your own home (we have no sales reps).
- You can order by **FREEPHONE** at any time **(0800 777911).**
- Your order is dispatched, fully insured by secure carrier, to your home within only a few days of ordering.

So why not try us? There is absolutely no risk in buying your wines from The International Wine Company. If, for any reason, you are not absolutely satisfied, you can return the wines within 14 days and owe us nothing.

Yours sincerely,

Graham A Tandy
Managing Director

PS *Your six FREE crystal glasses are perfect for almost every type of wine, from Claret to Chablis, from vin ordinaire to premier cru.*

The International Wine Company Limited, 6 The Cross, Enderby, Leicestershire LE9 5PF.
Registered in England No. 2643448 Telephone: 0533 752625 Fax: 0533 753700

4

Media 2 Speeches

Study Skills

This unit will develop your ability to analyse the structure and content of speeches. You'll gain practice in:

- **Looking at the different purposes of speeches** – Why do you think this person is giving a speech? What do they hope to achieve? Is there a dual purpose?
- **Working out the audience** – Who is the speech aimed at? How is the speech affected by and adapted for the specific audience?
- **Analysing the structure** – What progression is there in the speech? Think about how it opens and ends and what the significance is of both? How are points linked?
- **Examining the tone** – Consider how the speech sounds. Does it feel manipulative? An innocent and sincere sounding plea? Look carefully at the language used when considering this.

Speeches and the Media

Some people have predicted that in a media age, speeches will die out. They argue that politicians will use television, radio or the Internet to communicate in a more personal way with their audience. But that does not seem to be the case so far, and this unit looks in detail at the language of political speeches.

Use this first sample speech to explore some of the features of speeches.

The speech was delivered by the former British Prime Minister Margaret Thatcher. In it she wishes happy birthday to Ronald Reagan, former President of the USA.

Before you read the speech make some predictions. Bearing in mind that the speech is a birthday tribute:

- Will the tone be light-hearted or serious?
- Will it be formal or informal?
- Will it aim to entertain, inform or persuade?

Once you have examined the speech in more detail, look back at your responses to these questions.

....

Gala Birthday Tribute To President Ronald Reagan

by Baroness Margaret Thatcher

President Reagan, your excellencies, ladies and gentlemen, thank you for that wonderful introduction. It's the sort I would have loved at the beginning of every election campaign. It is an honour and a joy to be with you to celebrate the 44th anniversary of your 39th birthday.

Sir, you strode into our midst at a time when America needed you most. This great country had been through a period of national malaise bereft of any sense of moral direction. Through it all, throughout eight of the fastest moving years in memory, you were unflappable and unyielding.

You brushed off the jibes and jabs of your jealous critics. With that Irish twinkle and that easy homespun style, which never changed, you brought a new assurance to America. You were not only America's President – important as that is – you were a great leader. In a time of average men, you stood taller than anyone else.

With a toughness unseen for a long time, you stood face-to-face with the evil empire. And, with an unexpected diplomacy which confused your foes – and even some of your friends – you reached out to that empire, perhaps no longer evil, but still formidable. You met its leaders on their turf, but on your terms.

In a time of politicians, you proved yourself a statesman. And that leadership, that faith in freedom and enterprise brought about a renewal of this great country. America was back and the free world became a safer place.

It was not only that you were the Great Communicator – and you were the greatest – but that you had a message to communicate.

The message that had inspired the founding fathers, the message that has guided this nation from its birth – the essence of good government is to blend the wisdom of the ages with the circumstances of contemporary times – that is what you did. Not since Lincoln, or Winston Churchill in Britain, has there been a President who has so understood the power of words to uplift and to inspire.

....

1　Who is the audience for this speech? Does the audience appear to change from paragraph two onwards? Look closely at the text.

2　What picture of Ronald Reagan does the speech paint? Make a list of five of the qualities it ascribes to him.

3　Now look more closely at the vocabulary used. Look for examples of emotive words (words which have an emotional impact, such as *evil*). Look for examples of comparatives and superlatives. Why does the writer use these?

4　Look for any special effects – repetition of sounds (alliteration), or repetition of structures.

5　What do you like or dislike about the speech overall?

Comparing Speeches

Now compare two speeches. Both were made by American Presidents. The first is John F. Kennedy speaking in Berlin, a city which until the late 1980s was surrounded by a vast wall. Inside was a city committed to democracy; surrounding it was communist East Germany. Kennedy visits and preaches the message of democracy.

The second speech is by Bill Clinton, accepting nomination by the Democrats to stand as their candidate.

See what similarities and differences you notice.

Speech A:

The Proudest Boast
President John F. Kennedy, June 25, 1963

City Hall, West Berlin, Federal Republic of Germany

There are many people in the world who really don't understand, or say they don't, what is the great issue between the Free World and the Communist world. Let them come to Berlin. There are some who say that communism is the wave of the future. Let them come to Berlin. And there are some who say in Europe and elsewhere we can work with the Communists. Let them come to Berlin. And there are even a few who say that it's true that communism is an evil system, but it permits us to make economic progress. "Laßt sie nach Berlin kommen." Let them come to Berlin! Freedom has many difficulties and democracy is not perfect, but we have never had to put a wall up to keep our people in, to prevent them from leaving us.

...

You live in a defended island of freedom, but your life is part of the main. So let me ask you, as I close, to lift your eyes beyond the dangers of today to the hopes of tomorrow, beyond the freedom merely of this city of Berlin, or your country of Germany, to the advance of freedom everywhere, beyond the wall to the day of peace with justice, beyond yourselves and ourselves to all mankind.

Freedom is indivisible, and when one man is enslaved, all are not free. When all are free, then we can look forward to that day when this city will be joined as one, and this country, and this great Continent of Europe, in a peaceful and hopeful globe. When that day finally comes, as it will, the people of West Berlin can take sober satisfaction in the fact that they were in the front lines for almost two decades.

All free men, wherever they may live, are citizens of Berlin, and, therefore, as a free man, I take pride in the words "Ich bin ein Berliner."

Speech B:

President Bill Clinton accepts his nomination at the Democratic National Convention
August 29, 1996
Chicago, USA

Mr Chairman, Mr Vice President, my fellow Democrats, and my fellow Americans, thank you for your nomination. I don't know if I can find a fancy way to say this, but I accept.

Thank you.

My fellow Americans, this must be a campaign of ideas, not a campaign of insults. The American people deserve it. Now, here's the main idea. I love and revere the rich and proud history of America. And I am determined to take our best traditions into the future. But with all respect, we do not need to build a bridge to the past. We need to build a bridge to the future.

And that is what I commit to you to do.

So tonight, let us resolve to build that bridge to the 21st century, to meet our challenges and protect our values. Let us build a bridge to help our parents raise their children, to help young people and adults to get the education and training they need, to make our streets safer, to help Americans succeed at home and at work, to break the cycle of poverty and dependence, to protect our environment for generations to come, and to maintain our world leadership for peace and freedom. Let us resolve to build that bridge.

…

My fellow Americans 68 nights from tonight the American people will face once again a critical moment of decision. We're going to choose the last president of the 20th century and the first president of the 21st century.

But the real choice is not that. The real choice is whether we will build a bridge to the future or a bridge to the past; about whether we believe our best days are still out there or our best days are behind us; about whether we want a country of people all working together, or one where you're on your own.

Let us commit ourselves this night to rise up and build the bridge we know we ought to build all the way to the 21st century.

And let us have faith, faith, American faith, American faith that we are not leaving our greatness behind. We're going to carry it right on with us into that new century. A century of new challenge and unlimited promise.

Let us, in short, do the work that is before us, so that when our time here is over we will all watch the sun go down as we all must, and say truly, we have prepared our children for the dawn.

My fellow Americans, after these four good, hard years I still believe in the place called Hope – a place called America. Thank you. God bless you. And good night.

Following President Clinton's speech, imagine that a panel of experts analyse its strengths and weaknesses on television.

CRITIC A: Let's start with this speech, how would you rate the President's speech?

CRITIC B: I would give it a high rating. It was a powerful speech and a successful speech.

CRITIC A: Mark, what did you think? What kind of rating would you give the speech?

CRITIC C: I thought it was probably the best I've heard Bill Clinton speak, but it was still lacking in excitement. It read like a list of points. It didn't hang together.

CRITIC D: I'm not so sure. As a political speech, I thought it was adequate to good. But I don't think there were any parts here that people will really remember.

Activity

Now use the same format to compare the two presidents' speeches. Work in a group of three or four and imagine that you are analysing the way each speaker uses language.

You should try to comment on:

* Address to the audience
* The purpose
* Tone
* Vocabulary
* Sentences (questions, statements, commands?) (length of sentences)
* Special effects

Higher Level Techniques

Now look at some of the higher-level techniques speech-writers use to gain their effects.

Emmeline Pankhurst (1858–1928) was leader of the British Suffragettes. She campaigned fervently for women to have the right to vote but was met by strong opposition. In 1906, after a meeting with the British Prime Minister (Asquith) she despaired of women ever being granted the vote and resorted to more militant tactics. She was first arrested in the year of this speech – 1908.

....

Emmeline Pankhurst

Men politicians are in the habit of talking to women as if there were no laws that affect women. 'The fact is,' they say, 'the home is the place for women. Their interests are the rearing and training of children. These are the things that interest women. Politics have nothing to do with these things, and therefore politics do not concern women.' Yet the laws decide how women are to live in marriage,

how their children are to be trained and educated, and what the future of their children is to be. All that is decided by Act of Parliament. Let us take a few of these laws, and see what there is to say about them from the women's point of view.

First of all, let us take the marriage law. They are made by men for women. Let us consider whether they are equal, whether they are just, whether they are wise. What security of maintenance has the married woman? Many a married woman having given up her economic independence in order to marry, how is she compensated for that loss? What security does she get in that marriage for which she gave up economic independence? Take the case of a woman who has been earning a good income. She is told that she ought to give up her employment when she becomes a wife and a mother. What does she get in return? All that a married man is obliged by law to do for his wife is to provide for her shelter of some kind, food of some kind, and clothing of some kind. It is left to his good pleasure to decide what the shelter shall be, what the food shall be, what the clothing shall be. It is left to him to decide what money shall be spent on the home, and how it shall be spent; the wife has no voice legally in deciding any of these things. She has no legal claim upon any definite portion of his income. If he is a good man, a conscientious man, he does the right thing. If he is not, if he chooses almost to starve his wife, she has no remedy. What he thinks sufficient is what she has to be content with...

...I have spoken to you about the position of the married woman who does not exist legally as a parent, the parent of her own child. In marriage, children have one parent. Out of marriage children have also one parent. That parent is the mother – the unfortunate mother. She alone is responsible for the future of her child; she alone is punished if her child is neglected and suffers from neglect. But let me give you one illustration. I was in Herefordshire during the by-election. While I was there, an unmarried mother was brought before the bench of magistrates charged with having neglected her illegitimate child. She was a domestic servant, and had put the child out to nurse. The magistrates – there were colonels and landowners on that bench – did not ask what wages the mother got; they did not ask who the father was or whether he contributed to the support of the child. They sent that women to prison for three months for having neglected her child. I ask you women here tonight, if women had had some share in the making of laws, don't you think they would have found a way of making all fathers of such children equally responsible with the mothers for the welfare of those children?

Analysis

- How is it that Pankhurst's speech appears to be factual and informative rather than persuasive and biased? Why would this have suited her purpose and audience?

Look at how the first sentence is written as though it is a universally accepted fact rather than her opinion. She has distanced herself to avoid sounding too aggressive or personal; she sounds informative and avoids the use of the first person ('I'). Since we associate information with facts and facts with evidence we believe what she says is indisputable.

The first use of 'they' in the second sentence creates a type that is all men. 'They' all proclaim what suits women without actually ever consulting them. As the audience, we automatically question whether the home is really the place all women want to be and what right one group has of making decisions for another. To help you in your analysis think how different the response would have been if she had written:

> *'I am so sick and tired of the way all men treat women. They are all sexist, the whole lot of them. They think women should stay at home and that's all we're good for. What rubbish!'*

This is much more personal and emotional. Emmeline Pankhurst's aim was to persuade both men and women that women had the right to decide their own future; had the right to vote. Such a strong indictment of men would have alienated the very people she needed to help her cause. Certainly, it would not have commanded the intellectual respect that the first speech would. She understood that adopting the right style, tone and vocabulary is just as important as the content of your speech – if you want it to be successful.

Perhaps this would explain why it is often easier to write when you don't care passionately about the subject. It is a real challenge to write objectively and with control on a subject you care about. Try it and see.

What Makes a Good Speech?

In a group of four or five, discuss what you feel makes an effective speech. Come up with a list of features that an orator could follow as a guide and be 90% sure that they would produce a successful speech.

Consider the following:

- Meeting the needs of the audience
- Having an effective opening and thought-provoking ending
- Originality
- Use of language

Practice Makes Perfect...

Working with a partner, each of you write what you would consider to be a successful political speech.

Imagine you are trying to persuade staff and students at your school to move to a continental school day (8.30am – 2.30 pm); or that you are completely altering the uniform.

Based on your earlier exploration of the techniques of speech-making, come up with a really persuasive, entertaining piece.

You will then analyse the persuasiveness of your partner's speech. Read it through and consider your first impressions. Now, note down what persuasive techniques are used and how many times – keep a running total on each one. Next, look at P.A.S.T. (purpose, audience, structure, tone). How clear and effective are each of these? Finally, give the piece a mark out of 20 based on the following:

16+ = Excellent. Well-written, clear and persuasive. Thorough and comprehensive use of persuasive techniques and clear P.A.S.T.

14+ = Good. Generally sound and well organized. Lacked some originality and flair but good use of the techniques. Quite clear P.A.S.T. Would most likely be successful.

12+ = Satisfactory. Won't set the world alight or win prizes for the greatest ever speech but brought the point across and written clearly. Not all persuasive techniques employed successfully and P.A.S.T. not comprehensive.

10+ = Quite poor. Brief and lack of persuasiveness. Not fluent and lack of sufficient detail.

8+ = Well... not exactly the most effective speech ever!

Assignments

1   Find a speech that you like, either from this unit or from another source (*Penguin Book of Historic Speeches*, Hansard, Internet, etc.) and prepare it for performance. You will need to be methodical in your preparation. Follow the stages outlined below:

   • Read it through first of all to gain some general ideas. Next annotate the speech so that you can really start thinking what it is about and how it is organized.
   • Take a pencil and draw in lines as cut-off points where you feel there is a change of pace and/or tone. You will need to make these clear when you perform it.

51

- Ring words which need to be emphasized. Make line marks where you think you should pause for dramatic effect.
- Start learning the speech, a section of five lines at a time. Think about the image you want to portray

Perform to an audience and ask them to give you feedback. What did they think was the purpose of the speech? Was your presentation successful?

2 You are a prospective salesperson. You have joined a team that sell vacuum cleaners especially designed to suck up pet hair and remove all traces of odour. Write an imaginary sales pack that the company would send you. It needs to include the following:

- A letter congratulating you on making the right choice to be part of their team
- A suggested sample speech that you would make to companies when you visit them in order to persuade them to buy this product
- A suggested question and answer sheet to help you to understand how to answer the questions from a potential client whilst remaining persuasive and in control
- An example of the leaflet that your sales company sends out to prospective customers about the vacuum cleaner

Shakespeare

In this unit you will explore the various forms of language that Shakespeare employs in his plays, and gain an understanding of the concept of dramatic irony.

A* candidates will be able to make accurate and critical responses to Shakespeare texts, showing flair and precision in developing ideas about them. Their responses will make reference to structure and presentation and show originality in their interpretation and analysis.

Study Skills

- Understanding Shakespeare's use of public and private language
- Focusing on dramatic irony through the soliloquy
- Analysing the use of blank verse and prose
- Making subtle comparisons within and between Shakespearian texts

The Language of Shakespeare

William Shakespeare wrote plays that fall into three main categories: Comedies, Histories, and Tragedies. Within each genre and indeed within each play he carefully chose styles of language to fit the particular purpose of a character or to create a particular dramatic effect. It is these different styles that this unit will focus on.

Public Language

Henry V was written in 1599. To the surprise of his courtiers, the riotous Prince Hal (of *Henry IV*), now crowned as King Henry V, has become a noble statesman overnight. He promptly arrests three traitors and, taunted by a gift of tennis balls from the French prince – the Dauphin – he lays claim to the French throne and invades France. Heavily outnumbered, Henry must beat the French in battle to secure the port of Harfleurs. In the following extract from Act 3 Scene 1, Henry rallies his weary troops with an inspirational speech.

....

Henry V: Act 3, Scene 1

King Henry: Once more unto the breach, dear friends, once more;
Or close the wall up with our English dead.
In peace there's nothing so becomes a man
As modest stillness and humility;
But when the blast of war blows in our ears,   5
Then imitate the action of the tiger;

Stiffen the sinews, conjure up the blood,
Disguise fair nature with hard-favoured rage.
Then lend the eye a terrible aspect.
Let it pry through the portage of the head   10
Like the brass cannon; let the brow o'erwhelm it
As fearfully as doth a galled rock
O'erhang and jutty his confounded base,
Swilled with the wild and wasteful ocean.
Now set the teeth and stretch the nostril wide,   15
Hold hard the breath and bend up every spirit
To his full height. On, on you noblest English,
Whose blood is feat from fathers of war-proof!
Fathers that, like so many Alexanders,
Have in these parts from morn till even fought   20
And sheathed their swords for lack of argument.
Dishonour not your mothers; now attest
That those whom you called fathers did beget you.
Be copy now to men of grosser blood,
And teach them how to war. And you, good yeomen,   25
Whose limbs were made in England, show us here
The mettle of your pasture. Let us swear
That you are worth your breeding; which I doubt not;
For there is none of you so mean and base,
That hath not noble lustre in your eyes.   30
I see you stand like greyhounds in the slips,
Straining upon the start. The game's afoot:
Follow your spirit, and upon this charge
Cry 'God for Harry, England, and Saint George!'

Henry's speech is designed to motivate his men to attack and contains some of the key elements of persuasive language in:
- creating a 'kinship' with the audience
- employing emotive language (choosing words with an emotional impact, for example *terrible, blast of war*)
- having a rhythm that captures interest

Activity

1 Which words does Henry use to show kinship between himself and his soldiers?
2 What does Henry mean when he tells his men to *imitate the action of a tiger?* (line 6)
3 What does he mean when he compares his troops' fathers to *Alexanders?* (line 19) What effect do you suppose it would have on the men when Henry reminds them of their brave parents?
4 What image is created by Henry's simile *I see you stand like grey-*

hounds in the slips/Straining upon the start? (line 31)

5 Read the speech aloud and notice the rhythm of the words. How do you think this would help to persuade his soldiers to fight on?

6 Henry's last words invoke a battle cry that connects both himself and his countrymen to God. Why do you suppose he does this and what would it mean to his soldiers?

7 Henry tells his men to *Stiffen the sinews, conjure up the blood* (line 7). This is emotive language; it appeals to the emotions of the battle-weary men. Write down four other examples of emotive language that Henry uses and explain the meaning of each one.

8 The examples of emotive language that you will have found in Henry's speech sound very patriotic, but look closely at them. Everything the king asks his men to become is unnatural – they must dehumanize themselves in order to fight. Here are two possible interpretations of Henry's words:

Critic 1	Critic 2
Henry rouses the spirits in his men by glorifying war. He finds honour in their ability to kill, and is pleased with their bloodthirstiness.	Henry rouses the spirits of his men but really suggests that war is inhuman. In defeating the enemy, his soldiers must exaggerate their animal characteristics and quash their natural human ones.

Decide which critic you agree with and then write two paragraphs about how the language of the extract is designed to persuade. Refer to:

- kinship
- imagery
- emotive language
- the rhythm of the language

Intimate Language

Sometimes Shakespeare adapts his language to more intimate situations. Gone is the loud orator, stirring the emotions of his audience; instead quiet words are exchanged and the audience enters into the secrets imparted from one character to another on stage.

In *Measure for Measure* (written in 1604), the Duke of Vienna surrenders his power to his Deputy, Angelo, in the hope that he will clean up his corrupt state without the Duke having to play the tyrant himself. Angelo's first decision is dramatic – Claudio will be executed for getting his fiancée, Juliet, pregnant. Isabella, Claudio's sister, is summoned from her nunnery to plead with Angelo for her brother's life. Instead Angelo suggests that she have sex with him to save Claudio from execution. She vehemently refuses. The Duke returns disguised as Friar Lodowich and intervenes to save Claudio and expose Angelo. His deception requires

Isabella to believe that her brother has been killed. In this extract from Act 4 Scene 3, the Duke breaks this news to Isabella.

Measure for Measure: Act 4, Scene 3

Isabella: Ho, by your leave.
Duke: Good morning to you, fair and gracious daughter.
Isabella: The better given me by so holy a man.
          Hath yet the deputy sent my brother's pardon?
Duke: He hath released him, Isabel, from the world:
          His head is cut off, and sent to Angelo.
Isabella: Nay, but it is not so!
Duke: It is no other.
          Show your wisdom, daughter, in your close patience.
Isabella: Oh, I will to him and pluck out his eyes!
Duke: You shall not be admitted to his sight.
Isabella: Unhappy Claudio, wretched Isabel,
          Injurious world, most damned Angelo!
Duke: This nor hurts him nor profits you a jot.
          Forbear it therefore, give your cause to heaven.
          Mark what I say, which you shall find
          By every syllable a faithful verity:
          The Duke comes home tomorrow – nay, dry your eyes –
          One of our convent, and his confessor,
          Gives me this instance. Already he hath carried
          Notice to Escalus and Angelo,
          Who do prepare to meet him at the gates,
          There to give up their power. If you can pace your wisdom
          In that good path that I would wish it go,
          And you shall have your bosom on this wretch,
          Grace of the Duke, revenges to your heart,
          And general honour.
Isabella: I am directed by you.
Duke: This letter then to Friar Peter give,
          'Tis that he sent me of the Duke's return.
          Say by this token I desire his company
          At Mariana's house tonight. Her cause and yours
          I'll perfect him withal, and he shall bring you
          Before the Duke; and to the head of Angelo
          Accuse him home and home. For my poor self,
          I am combined by a sacred vow
          And shall be absent. Wend you with this letter:
          Command these fretting waters from your eyes
          With a light heart; trust not my holy order
          If I pervert your course.

1   Why do you think Isabella refers to the Duke as *so holy a man*?
2   Look at the familiar terms which the Duke uses to address Isabella: *fair and gracious daughter; Isabel; daughter.* Why does he do this?
3   What impression do you get of the Duke's attitude towards her? Look at the way he gives information: *His head is cut off, and sent to Angelo; Mark what I say;* and at her response at the end: *I am directed by you.*
What does this show about the way he manipulates Isabella's reactions?
4   Isabella believes she has lost her brother. She is deceived in her simple trust in the 'Friar', and is prepared to be 'directed' by him. What is it that he tells her to do?
5   What is ironic about the Friar's claim that every syllable he utters will be a *faithful verity*?
6   The Friar has laid a plan to catch out Angelo. What then is also ironic about his last words *trust not my holy order/If I pervert your course*?
7   Using your notes on this short extract write two paragraphs on your impressions of the Duke. Use quotations from the extract to support your views.

Assignment

Focusing on the extracts from *Henry V* and *Measure for Measure*, write an essay on the differences between public and intimate language in Shakespeare's plays. You should consider:
•   the way in which the speakers speak
•   the intention behind their words
•   imagery
•   deception
•   dramatic irony

Soliloquies

Often in Shakespeare's plays, a character will stand on stage alone and think out loud. This is called a soliloquy. It is a dramatic device that allows the audience insight into certain characteristics or motives that are not revealed to the other characters. It is the point at which each character exhibits their true feelings and personality.

In *Hamlet* (written in 1602), the young Prince of Denmark is visited by the ghost of his father, who tells him that it was Hamlet's uncle, the newly crowned Claudius, who killed him. To make matters worse, Claudius has taken Gertrude, Hamlet's mother, as his wife. The ghost asks Hamlet to revenge his foul and most unnatural murder, but Hamlet does not find this an easy task. In this extract from Act 2 Scene 2 he begins to

Key term

Dramatic Irony occurs when the audience knows more than one or all of the characters on stage.

question his own bravery and sense of duty.

....

Hamlet: Act 2, Scene 2

Hamlet: Am I a coward?
Who calls me villain? Breaks my pate across,
Plucks off my beard and blows it in my face?
Tweaks me by the nose? Gives me the lie i'th' throat
As deep as to the lungs? Who does me this?   5
Ha, 'swounds, I should take it. For it cannot be
But I am pigeon-livered and lack gall
To make oppression bitter, or ere this
I should ha' fatted all the region kites
With this slave's offal. Bloody, bawdy villain!   10
Remorseless, treacherous, lecherous, kindless villain!
O, vengeance!
Why, what an ass am I! This is most brave,
That I, the son of a dear father murdered,
Prompted to my revenge by heaven and hell,   15
Must like a whore unpack my heart with words
And fall a-cursing like a very drab,
A stallion! Fie upon't, foh!
About, my brains. Hum – I have heard
That guilty creatures sitting at a play   20
Have by the very cunning of the scene
Been struck so to the soul that presently
They have proclaimed their malefactions.
For murder, though it have no tongue, will speak
With most miraculous organ. I'll have these players   25
Play something like the murder of my father
Before mine uncle. I'll observe his looks.
I'll tent him to the quick. If 'a do blench,
I know my course. The spirit that I have seen
May be a devil, and the devil hath power   30
T'assume a pleasing shape, yea, and perhaps
Out of my weakness and my melanchoy,
As he is very potent with such spirits,
Abuses me to damn me. I'll have grounds
More relative than this. The play's the thing   35
Wherein I'll catch the King.

....

Activity   1   What does Hamlet mean when he says he *should ha' fatted all the
                 region kites/With this slave's offal*? (lines 9–10) Who is the *slave* that
                 Hamlet refers to?

2 What plan does Hamlet devise to test the guilt of Claudius?

3 Why does Hamlet feel he must verify Claudius' guilt?

4 What does Hamlet think of himself at the beginning of this speech?

5 In this soliloquy alone, Hamlet says that his father was murdered and that he is a coward for not having avenged this, but also says that the ghost may have been the devil trying to trick him. In your opinion, is Hamlet a coward, or is he being sensible in his delay?

6 Write a response to the following question:

Why is it necessary that Hamlet gives this speech in the form of a soliloquy?

Refer to:

- its dramatic effect
- what it reveals of Hamlet's character
- what it reveals of other characters

Assignment

In the play *Macbeth* (written in 1606), a loyal Thane, who has just distinguished himself in battle, is told by witches that he will one day become King of Scotland. Confused but intrigued by this information he writes to his wife telling her of the prophecy. She looks forward to her husband's homecoming and the impending visit of Duncan, the present king.

Compare the two extracts below from *Macbeth*. What does each one tell you about the character who speaks? How does the language evoke a sense of evil or fear? Who appears to be the stronger of the two characters? How do Lady Macbeth's ideas for the impending doom of King Duncan compare to her husband's? Write an essay on Shakespeare's characterization as revealed by these two soliloquies.

Macbeth: Act 1, Scene 5

Lady Macbeth: The raven himself is hoarse
That croaks the fatal entrance of Duncan
Under my battlements. Come, you spirits
That tend on mortal thought, unsex me here;
And fill me, from the crown to the toe, top-full
Of direst cruelty! Make thick my blood,
Stop up the access and passage to remorse,
That no compunctious visitings of nature
Shake my fell purpose, nor keep peace between
The effect and it! Come to my woman's breasts,
And take my milk for gall, you murdering ministers,
Wherever in your sightless substances
You wait on nature's mischief! Come, thick night,
And pall thee in the dunnest smoke of hell,
That my keen knife see not the wound it makes,

Nor Heaven peep through the blanket of the dark,
To cry, Hold, hold!

....

Macbeth: Act 1, Scene 7

Macbeth: If it were done when 'tis done, then 'twere well
It were done quickly. If the assassination
Could trammel up the consequence, and catch,
With his surcease, success; that but this blow
Might be the be-all and the end-all here,
But here, upon this bank and shoal of time –
We'd jump the life to come. But in these cases
We still have judgment here; that we but teach
Bloody instructions, which being taught, return
To plague the inventor: this even-handed justice
Commands the ingredients of our poison'd chalice
To our own lips. He's here in double trust:
First, as I am his kinsman and his subject,
Strong both against the deed: then, as his host,
Who should against his murderer shut the door,
Not bear the knife myself. Besides, this Duncan
Hath borne his faculties so meek, hath been
So clear in his great office, that his virtues
Will plead like angels, trumpet-tongued, against
The deep damnation of his taking-off;
And pity, like a new-born babe,
Striding the blast, or heaven's cherubin, hors'd
Upon the sightless couriers of the air,
Shall blow the horrid deed in every eye,
That tears shall drown the wind. – I have no spur
To prick the sides of my intent, but only
Vaulting ambition, which o'erleaps itself,
And falls on the other.

....

Blank Verse

All of Shakespeare's language studied so far has been in the form of blank verse. Indeed this is the most frequently used form in Shakespeare's plays and is characterized by these features:
• It looks like poetry on the page
• It has a particular rhythm; each line contains 10 syllables

(5 alternately weak and strong syllables, though you will notice that Shakespeare does not keep to this rigidly at all times)
- It does not rhyme
- It mimics the rhythm of English conversation

Its form also helped Shakespeare's actors to learn their lines!

As an example, read this brief extract from *Twelfth Night*. The Duke Orsino is listening to music to indulge his lovesickness:

Twelfth Night: Act 2, Scene 4

Orsino: Now good Cesario, but that piece of song,
That old and antic song we heard last night.
Methought it did relieve my passion much,
More than light airs and recollected terms
Of these most brisk and giddy-paced times.

Activity

Read the lines out aloud to get the strong/weak rhythm, then write them down showing the strong and weak syllables using the symbols below. The first two lines have been done for you.

✗ ╱ ✗ ╱ ✗ ╱ ✗ ╱ ✗ ╱
Now good Ce sa rio but that piece of song,

✗ ╱ ✗ ╱ ✗ ╱ ✗ ╱ ✗ ╱
That old and an tic song we heard last night.

✗ = weak (unstressed)
╱ = strong (stressed)

You may have noted that in the last line Shakespeare splits the syllables of paced to make two sounds – pace and -èd, so that the line contains the required 10 syllables. Look at the lines below and mark the stressed and unstressed syllables using the symbols above:

Antonio: Taught him to face me out of his acquaintance,
And grew a twenty years' removed thing.
Orsino: Him will I tear out that cruel eye
Where he sits crowned in his master's spite.

This particular blank verse is technically known as **iambic pentameter**. Sometimes, however, Shakespeare discards verse for prose.

Prose

As You Like It (written in 1600) is set in the Forest of Arden, where Duke Senior and his court enjoy life. Orlando who has fled the Duchy of Frederick to escape his murderous brother is caught hanging love poems on trees by Rosalind who has also fled from Duke Frederick. Rosalind is disguised as a low-born man 'Ganymede'. When Orlando and Jaques enter on stage, she and Celia hide, and listen to the men talk of love. Orlando confesses his feelings for Rosalind. In this extract, 'Ganymede' emerges from the trees and offers Orlando assistance with his lovesickness:

••

As You Like It: Act 3, Scene 2

Rosalind: Love is merely a madness, and I tell you, deserves as well a dark house and a whip as madmen do; and the reason why they are not so punished and cured is that lunacy is so ordinary that the whippers are in love too. Yet I profess curing it by counsel.

Orlando: Did you ever cure any so?

Rosalind: Yes, one; and in this manner. He was to imagine me his love, his mistress; and I set him every day to woo me. At which time would I, being but a moonish youth, grieve, be effeminate, changeable, longing and liking, proud, fantastical, apish, shallow, inconstant, full of tears, full of smiles; for every passion something, and for no passion truly anything, as boys and women are for the most part cattle of this colour – would now like him, now loathe him; then entertain him, then forswear him; now weep for him, then spit at him, that I drave my suitor from his mad humour of love, to a living humour of madness, which was to forswear the full stream of the world and to live in a nook merely monastic. And thus I cured him, and this will I take upon me to wash your liver as clean as a sound sheep's heart, that there shall not be one spot of love in't.

Orlando: I would not be cured, youth.

Rosalind: I would cure you if you would but call me Rosalind and come every day to my cot, and woo me.

Orlando: Now by the faith of my love, I will. Tell me where it is.

Rosalind: Go with me to it, and I'll show it you. And by the way you shall tell me where in the forest you live. Will you go?

Orlando: With all my heart, good youth.

Rosalind: Nay, you must call me Rosalind. – Come, sister. Will you go?

Activity

1 Rosalind deceives Orlando by relating a tale of how she once cured a lovesick boy of his feelings. Why do you suppose prose is better suited to this purpose than verse? You should consider:
   - the length of his tale
   - the manner in which he relates his changing emotions
2 Rosalind speaks in prose in order to emphasize the lower status of her assumed character Ganymede, and this helps to make the scene comic. Identify images used to suggest her rustic background.

There is comedy in the on-stage deception of Rosalind dressed as a man, but there is equal comic value in the way Shakespeare teases all women as he lightheartedly examines their supposed fickleness.

3 Reread Rosalind's speech on how she once cured a man of his lovesickness. Write a list of all the different ways she treated him, and of the different emotions she exhibited towards him. You will see there is little wonder in the man eventually going mad.
4 Ganymede lays down some rules for the 'cure': (a) *I would cure you if you would but call me Rosalind and come every day to my cot, and woo me.* (b) *And by the way you shall tell me where in the forest you live.* (c) *Nay, you must call me Rosalind.* Why would these rules be considered comic in the theatre?
5 Write a modernized version of this scene paying attention to retaining the humour in it.

Assignment

Verse and prose can be used by the same character in a single play, for different purposes. For example, King Henry uses verse form to inspire his troops, but when he is in disguise, or talking informally to them, he uses more 'common' prose language in order to be closer socially to them.

In another of Shakespeare's plays, *Othello*, a Moor is a respected soldier and leader. He is newly wed to Desdemona, and has promoted Cassio to lieutenant for his help in wooing her. However, in so doing, he has overlooked Iago's claim to the post. Iago wants revenge and will use Roderigo's unrequited love for Desdemona to help get it.

Read the extracts and then write an essay on the different forms of language Iago employs. Consider when he uses verse and when prose, and what effect this has on our appreciation of his character.

Othello: Act 1, Scene 3

Roderigo: Iago.
Iago: What sayst thou, noble heart?
Roderigo: What will I do, think'st thou?
Iago: Why go to bed and sleep.

Roderigo: I will incontinently drown myself.

Iago: I' thou dost, I shall never love thee after. Why, thou silly gentleman!

Roderigo: It is silliness to live when to live is torment; and then have we a prescription to die when death is our physician.

Iago: O, villainous! I ha' looked upon the world for four times seven years, and since I could distinguish betwixt a benefit and an injury I never found man that knew how to love himself. Ere I would say I would drown myself for the love of a guinea hen, I would change my humanity for a baboon.

Roderigo: What should I do? I confess it is my shame to be so fond, but it is not in my virtue to amend it.

Iago: Virtue? A fig! 'Tis in ourselves that we are thus or thus. Our bodies are our gardens, to the which our wills are gardeners; so that if we will plant nettles or sow lettuce, set hysop and weed up thyme, supply it with one gender of herbs or distract it with many, either to have it sterile with idleness or manured with industry, why, the power and corrigible authority of this lies in our wills. If the beam of our lives had not one scale of reason to peise another of sensuality, the blood and baseness of our natures would conduct us to most preposterous conclusions. But we have reason to cool our raging motions, our carnal stings, our unbitted lusts; whereof I take this that you call love to be a sect or scion.

Roderigo: It cannot be.

Iago: It is merely a lust of the blood and a permission of the will. Come, be a man. Drown thyself? Drown cats and blind puppies. I have professed me thy friend, and I confess me knit to thy deserving with cables of perdurable toughness. I could never better stead thee than now. Put money in thy purse. Follow thou the wars, defeat thy favour with an usurped beard. I say, put money in thy purse. It cannot be long that Desdemona should continue her love to the Moor – put money in thy purse – nor he his to her. It was a violent commencement in her, and thou shalt see an answerable sequestration – put but money in thy purse. These Moors are changeable in their wills – fill thy purse with money. The food that to him now is as luscious as locusts shall be to him shortly as bitter as coloquintida. She must change for youth. When she is sated with his body, she will find the error of her choice. Therefore put money in thy purse. If thou wilt needs damn thyself, do it a more delicate way than drowning. Make all the money thou canst. If sanctimony and a frail vow betwixt and erring barbarian and a super-subtle Venetian be not too hard for my wits and all the tribe of hell, thou shalt enjoy her; therefor make money. A pox o' drowning thyself – it is clean out of the way. Seek though rather to be hanged in compassing thy joy than to be drowned and go without her.

Roderigo: Wilt thou be fast to my hopes if I depend on the issue?

Iago: Thou art sure of me. Go, make money. I have told thee often, and I re-tell thee again and again, I hate the Moor. My cause is hearted, thine hath no less reason. Let us be conjunctive in our revenge against him. If thou canst cuckold him, thou dost thyself a pleasure, me a sport. There are many events in the womb of time, which will be delivered. Traverse, go provide thy money. We will have more of this tomorrow. Adieu.

Roderigo: Where shall we meet i'th' morning?

Iago: At my lodging.

Roderigo: I'll be with you betimes.

Iago: Go to, farewell –
Do you hear, Roderigo?

Roderigo: I'll sell all my land. EXIT

Iago: Thus do I ever make my fool my purse –
For I mine own gained knowledge should profane
If I would time expend with such a snipe
But for my sport and profit. I hate the Moor,
And it is thought abroad that 'twixt my sheets
He has done my office. I know not if't be true,
But I, for mere suspicion in that kind,
Will do as if for surety. He holds me well:
The better shall my purpose work on him.

Cassio's a proper man. Let me see now,
To get his place, and to plume up my will
In double knavery – how, how? Let's see.
After some time to abuse Othello's ears
That he is too familiar with his wife;
He hath a person and a smooth dispose
To be suspected, framed to make women false.
The Moor is of a free and open nature,
That thinks men honest that but seem to be so,
And will as tenderly be led by the nose
As asses are.
I ha't, it is engendered; Hell and night
Must bring this monstrous birth to the world's light.

Othello: Act 2, Scene 1

Iago: (to an attendant as he goes out) Do thou meet me presently at the harbour. (To Roderigo) Come hither. If thou beest valiant – as they say base me in love have then a nobility in their natures more than is native to them – list me. The lieutenant tonight watches on the court of guard. First, I must tell thee this: Desdemona is directly in love with him.

Roderigo: With him? Why, 'tis not possible!

Iago: Lay thy finger thus, and let thy soul be instructed.Mark me with what violence she first loved the Moor, but for bragging and telling her fantastical lies. To love him still for prating? – let now thy discreet heart think it. Her eye must be fed, and what delight shall she have to look on the devil? When the blood is made dull with the act of sport, there should be again to inflame it, and to give satiety a fresh appetite, loveliness in favour, sympathy in yeas, manners, and beauties, all which the Moor is defective in. Now, for want of these requires conveniences, her delicate tenderness will find itself abused, begin to heave the gorge, disrelish and abhor the Moor. Very nature will instruct her in it and compel her to some second choice. Now, sir, this granted – as it is a most pregnant and unforced position – who stands so eminent in the degree of this fortune as Cassio does? – a knave very voluble, no further conscionable than in putting on the mere form of civil and humane seeming for the better compass of his salt and most hidden loose affection. Why, none; why, none – a slipper and subtle knave, a finder of occasion, that has an eye can stamp and counterfeit advantages, though true advantage never present itself, a devilish knave! Besides, the knave is handsome, young, and hath all those requisites in him that folly and green minds look after. A pestilient complete knave, and the women hath found him already.

Roderigo: I cannot believe that in her. She's full of most blessed condition.

Iago: Blessed fig's end! The wine she drinks is made of grapes. If she had been blessed, she would never have loved the Moor. Blessed pudding! Didst thou not see her paddle with the palm of his hand? Didst not mark that?

Roderigo: Yes, that I did, but that was but courtesy.

Iago: Lechery, by this hand; an index and obscure prologue to the history of lust and foul thoughts. They met so near with their lips and their breaths emtraced together. Villainous thought Roderigo! When these mutualities so marshal the way, hard at hand comes the master and main exercise, th'incorporate conclusion. Pish! But, sir, you be ruled by me. I have brought you from Venice. Watch you tonight. For the command, I'll lay it upon you. Cassio knows you not; I'll not be far from you. Do you find some occasion to anger Cassio, either by speaking too loud, or tainting his discipline, or from what other course you please, which the time shall more favourable minister.

Roderigo: Well.

Iago: Sir, he's rash and very sudden in choler, and haply may strike at you. Provoke him that he may, for even out of that will I cause these of Cyprus to mutiny, whose qualification shall come into no true taste again but by the displanting of Cassio. So shall you have a shorter journey to your desires by the means I shall then have to prefer them, and the impediment most profitably removed, without the which there were no expectation of your prosperity.

Roderigo: I will do this, if you can bring it to any opportunity.

Iago: I warrant thee. Meet me by and by at the citadel. I must fetch his necessities ashore. Farewell.　　　　EXIT

Roderigo: Adieu.

Iago: That Cassio loves her, I do well believe it.
That she loves him, 'tis apt and of great credit.
The Moor – howbe't that I endure him not –
is of a constant, loving, noble nature,
And I dare to think he'll prove to Desdemona
A most dear husband. Now I do love her too,
Not out of absolute lust – though peradventure
I stand accountant for as great a sin –
But partly led to diet my revenge
For that I do suspect the lusty Moor
Hath leapt into my seat, the thought whereof
Doth, like a poisonous mineral, gnaw my inwards;
And nothing can or shall content my soul
Till I am evened with him, wife for wife –
Or failing so, yet that I put the Moor
At least into a jealousy so strong
That judgement cannot cure, which thing to do,
If this poor trash of Venice whom I trace
For his quick hunting stand the putting on,
I'll have our Michael Cassio on the hip,
Abuse him to the Moor in the rank garb –
For I fear Cassio in my nightcap, too –
Make the Moor thank me, love me and reward me
For making him egregiously an ass,
And practising his peace and quiet
Even to madness. 'Tis here, but yet confused.

6

Comparative Study: The Short Story

When studying the short story the A* candidate is expected to know something of the social significance of the text, to analyse the narrative form and discuss why it appeals to the reader, and you also need to look in depth at the patterns and details of language.

Study Skills

- Analysing how the short story differs from the novel
- Understanding the structure of the short story
- Focusing on the language and plot development of the short story

Comparing the Novel and the Short Story

In many ways, studying the short story is similar to studying the novel. Both texts contain the same central elements – characterization, plot, and setting. However, the short story is different from the novel in important respects.

- The short story relates the tale of only one main event
- It uses only a limited number of characters
- It goes almost immediately into the action
- The background to the story is only lightly sketched
- There is usually a 'twist in the tale' at the end

Setting

In a novel the writer has space to spend time establishing firm setting and characterization. The short story writer does not have this luxury.

Read the opening two texts, A and B, below. One is the introduction to a short story, the other to a novel. As you read, begin to analyse the setting and consider how important this might be to each plot.

· ·

A To the red country and part of the grey country of Oklahoma the last rains came gently, and they did not cut the scarred earth. The ploughs crossed and re-crossed the rivulet marks. The last rains lifted the corn quickly and scattered weed colonies and grass along the sides of the roads so that the grey country and the dark red country began to disappear under a green cover. In the last part of May the sky grew pale and the clouds that had hung in high puffs

for so long in the spring were dissipated. The sun flared down on the growing corn day after day until a line of brown spread along the edge of each green bayonet. The clouds appeared, and went away, and in a while they did not try any more. The weeds grew darker green to protect themselves, and they did not spread any more. The surface of the earth crusted, a thin hard crust, and as the sky became pale, so the earth became pale, pink in the red country and white in the grey country.

In the water-cut gullies the earth dusted down in dry little streams. Gophers and ant lions started small avalanches. And as the sharp sun struck day after day, the leaves of the young corn became less stiff and erect; they bent in a curve at first, and then, as the central ribs of strength grew weak, each leaf tilted downward. Then it was June, and the sun shone more fiercely. The brown lines on the corn leaves widened and moved in on the central ribs. The weeds frayed and edged back towards their roots. The air was thin and the sky more pale; and every day the earth paled.

B Beneath the great grey cliff of Clogher Mor there was a massive square black rock, dotted with white limpets, sitting in the sea. The sea rose and fell about it frothing. Rising, the sea hoisted the seaweed that grew along the rock's rims until the long red winding strands spread like streams of blood through the white foam. Falling, the tide sucked the strands down taut from their bulbous roots.

Activity

1 Complete the table below, considering how setting is conveyed in each extract.

	Text A	Text B
Descriptions of colours		
Descriptions of movement		
Descriptions of nature		

2 Both extracts introduce the reader to the place in which the action will take place. From the evidence of the second extract, and the information in your chart, would you expect Text B to be an introduction to a novel or a short story? Give three reasons for your decision.

Plot

The two texts have similar beginnings. Text A is from the novel, *The Grapes of Wrath* by John Steinbeck and Text B is from the short story, *The Wounded Cormorant* by Liam O'Flaherty. Now look at this in more depth to discover other features that distinguish the short story from the novel. However, before you read more of *The Wounded Cormorant*, what do you predict is going to happen?

....

The Wounded Cormorant

Silence. It was noon. The sea was calm. Rock-birds slept on its surface, their beaks resting on their fat white breasts. Tall sea-gulls standing on one leg dozed high up in the ledges of the cliff. On the great rock there was a flock of black cormorants resting, bobbing their long necks to draw the food from their swollen gullets.

Above on the cliff-top a yellow goat was looking down into the sea. She suddenly took fright. She snorted and turned towards the crag at a smart turn. Turning, her hoof loosed a flat stone from the cliff's edge. The stone fell, whirling, on to the rock where the cormorants rested. It fell among them with a crash and arose in fragments. The birds swooped into the air. As they rose a fragment of stone struck one of them in the right leg. The leg was broken. The wounded bird uttered a shrill scream and dropped the leg. As the bird flew outwards from the rock the leg dangled crookedly.

The flock of cormorants did not fly far. As soon as they passed the edge of the rock they dived headlong into the sea. Their long, black bodies, with outstretched necks, passed rapidly beneath the surface of the waves, a long way, before they rose again, shaking the brine from their heads. Then they sat in the sea, their pale brown throats thrust forward, their tiny heads poised on their curved long necks. They sat watching, like upright snakes, trying to discover whether there were enemies near. Seeing nothing, they began to cackle and flutter their feathers. But the wounded one rushed about in the water flapping its wings in agony.

....

Activity

1   How much actually happens in a short story? How much plot is there? Use the graph below to chart the incidence of action in *The Wounded Cormorant* against the plot pattern of the *The Grapes of Wrath* extract.

The Grapes of Wrath

High

Medium

Low

None

| *The Grapes of Wrath* | 1st para. | | 2nd para. | |
| *The Wounded Cormorant* | 1st para. | 2nd para. | 3rd para. | 4th para. |

71

2   Select one sentence from each paragraph of *The Wounded Cormorant* that describes the main action. The first has been done for you.

1st para: Rising, the sea hoisted the seaweed that grew along the rock's rims until the long red winding strands spread like streams of blood through the white foam.

2nd para:

3rd para:

4th para:

3   The 'action' in the story happens very quickly. Paragraph 3 contains the main plot; the rest of the story follows up on this one incident. Other surrounding information is kept firmly in the background; for example, it is the goat's fault that the stone is dislodged, but the reader is never told what frightened it into turning sharply on the cliff edge.
- Why do you suppose O'Flaherty omits this detail?
- Are there other examples of where he keeps 'background information' to a minimum?

Character

There are no human characters in *The Wounded Cormorant*, but we are swiftly introduced to the animal characters: the goat, the injured cormorant, and the group of birds which are never described individually.

Activity   Reread the extract on pages 70–1 and then respond to these questions.
1   Why do you think O'Flaherty describes the actions of the rest of the flock, compared to the wounded bird?
2   What is the effect of describing the flock as *upright snakes*?
3   How do you predict the birds will act next?

Read the ending of the short story and see how accurate your prediction is:

… They fell upon it fiercely, tearing at its body with their beaks, plucking out its black feathers and rooting it about with their feet. It struggled madly to creep farther on the ledge, trying to get into a dark crevice in the cliff to hide, but they dragged it back again and pushed it towards the brink of the ledge. One bird prodded its right eye with its beak. Another gripped the broken leg firmly in its beak and tore at it.

At last the wounded bird lay on its side and began to tremble, offering no resistance to their attacks. Then they cackled loudly and, dragging it to the brink of the ledge they hurled it down. It fell fluttering feebly through the air, slowly descending, turning round and round, closing and opening its wings, until it reached the sea.

Then it fluttered its wings twice and lay still. An advancing wave dashed it against the side of the black rock and then it disappeared, sucked down among the seaweed strands.

Comparing Short Stories

We have looked briefly at the essential elements of the short story – its one main event, few characters, economical background sketches, its quick movement into the action; and its twist in the tale. Now compare two more short stories.

Read the introductions to *Mrs Pulaska* by Christopher Burns and *My Good Fairy* by Christopher Hope and consider how well they fulfil the ingredients of the short story.

••

Mrs Pulaska

No one knew where she came from, or why she had sought refuge among us. Perhaps she yearned for the tiny villages and small farms of her childhood, now denied to her for ever by the forces of history; perhaps she merely sought escape.

For people such as us she was an emissary from an unknown world, a bizarre and oddly self-absorbed stranger with a heavy accent. The very planes and set of her face were different to the ones we were used to. She was angular, with bony features and protuberant eyes and long black hair like a witch's. For my schoolfriends and me she was a figure of both fear and scorn; we even imagined that she might be German, and to us all Germans were still enemies.

But her name was Mrs Pulaska, and she was Polish. Of Mr Pulaska, or of a wedding ring, there was no sign. For the time she was with us she lived in a tiny room at the back of the butcher's shop in the village. It must have been narrow and damp, but from the solitary window she could look out across fields and towards the hills. Because she always looked cold and undernourished the shopkeepers gave her scraps of meat or the occasional vegetable, despite rationing. She wore black clothes even in summer, always with gloves; in winter she wore mittens, boots, and what looked like an outsize greatcoat scavenged from the remnants of an unidentified army.

When she began to come to our farm I felt both threatened and guilty. There had been no need for me to think such terrible things about Mrs Pulaska, I decided, for I feared that in some obscure way she had come to take revenge.

My Good Fairy

Nicodemus was a big giver. And this was odd, him being so skinny. His tunic was cut square across his chest and there seemed next to nothing to the guy. Just these little arms and his legs in the long baggy shorts narrowing from the knee to little rocky ankles. His fuzz of black beard was blacker than his face. He didn't even have much to say, just 'yes' and 'no', and 'take this my little lord'. He looked like nothing but then he'd wink or clap and suddenly something would appear.

He came with the house. If he hadn't coughed when we went into the garage, 'I'd never have found him!' my father told Gus Trupshaw. He was stored in the darkness along with a blue Rudge bicycle frame without wheels, a wooden clothes-horse, two broken ladders, a case of Trotter's jellies 'from the heart of South Africa' – lime green and as hard as cakes of soap because the damp had got to them – and an advertisement for New Consolidated Goldfields which included among its directors Sir G. S. Harvie-Watt, Bt., TD, QC, MP. I used to say the name when I was in bed and sleep wouldn't come and I thought of vampires and death.

••

Activity

1   When do you think *Mrs Pulaska* is set? Give textual evidence to support your thoughts.

2   *I used to say the name when I was in bed and sleep wouldn't come and I thought of vampires and death.* How does this line add to the idea that this is a childhood memory?

3   Both Nicodemus and Mrs Pulaska are seen as being outside their community. How is this achieved? Use quotations from the texts as evidence.

4   In *Mrs Pulaska* in particular, the community appears to be very tightly

knit and wary of outsiders. How does this differ from the feeling the narrator portrays towards Nicodemus?

5 Whilst the boy in *The Good Fairy* seems to have had a good relationship with Nicodemus, certain phrases point to the way he is regarded as a commodity or possession. Which parts of the text suggest this?

6 Look at types of things that Nicodemus is 'stored' with. What do they all have in common? What might this suggest about the servant?

7 Why do you suppose Mrs Pulaska always wears black? Why does she always wear mittens? Given that she is a Polish emigrant from the war, what might she be trying to hide?

8 Both characters are outsiders:
• *For people like us she was an emissary from an unknown world.*
• *He looked like nothing, but then he'd wink or clap and suddenly something would appear.*

From these two quotations, predict what sort of plot might unfold in the two stories.

Both extracts require close reading, not so much of the text itself, but of the meanings behind the words. This is another key skill of the short story writer; to lend additional layers of meaning to a story not just through what is said, but in what is merely suggested.

Assignment

Write a comparison of the two opening sequences. What do these introductions have in common? What sets them apart from each other? You should consider:
• the role of each narrator
• the portrayal of central and minor characters
• the setting
• the time in which they are set and any social/historical details that are relevant.

The Language of Short Stories

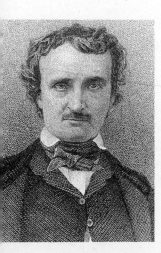

Edgar Allan Poe (1809–49) is thought by many to be the father of the short story, and he has had a great influence on the modern horror genre.

The following extract is the conclusion to Poe's short story, *The Black Cat.* In it, the narrator, who loves his pet cat, comes to hate it and eventually kills it. An almost replica cat then finds its way into his house. The narrator goes to kill this animal also, but as his wife tries to stop him, he kills her instead. This, he thinks, has scared the cat off, and he sets about entombing his wife's body behind a wall in his cellar.

Read this extract. Look at how his choice of language anchors the story in a specific time and place and how it creates a particular feeling or atmosphere.

The Black Cat

Upon the fourth day of the assassination, a party of the police came, very unexpectedly, into the house, and procured again to make rigorous investigation of the premises. Secure, however, in the inscrutability of my place of concealment, I felt no embarrassment whatever. The officers bade me accompany them in their search. They left no nook or corner unexplored. At length, for the third or fourth time, they descended into the cellar. I quivered not in a muscle. My heart beat calmly as that of one who slumbers in innocence. I walked the cellar end to end. I folded my arms upon my bosom, and roamed easily to and fro. The police were thoroughly satisfied and prepared to depart. The glee at my heart was too strong to be restrained. I burned to say if but one word, by way of triumph, and to render doubly sure their assurance of my guiltlessness.

'Gentlemen,' I said at last, as the party ascended the steps, 'I delight to have allayed your suspicions. I wish you all health, and a little more courtesy. By the bye, gentlemen, this – this is a very well constructed house.' (In the rabid desire to say something easily, I scarcely knew what I uttered at all.) – 'I may say an excellently well constructed house. These walls – are you going gentlemen? – these walls are solidly put together,' and here, through the mere frenzy of bravado, I rapped heavily, with a cane which I held in my hand, upon that very portion of the brick-work behind which stood the corpse of the wife of my bosom.

But may God shield and deliver me from the fangs of the Arch-fiend! No sooner had the reverberation of my blows sunk into silence, than I was answered by a voice from within the tomb! – by a cry, at first muffled and broken, like the sobbing of a child, and then quickly swelling into one long, loud, and continuous scream, utterly anomalous and inhuman – a howl – a wailing shriek, half of horror and half of triumph, such as might have arisen only out of hell, conjointly from the throats of the damned in their agony and of the demons that exalt in damnation.

Of my own thoughts it is folly to speak. Swooning, I staggered to the opposite wall. For one instant the party upon the stair remained motionless, through extremity of terror and of awe. In the next, a dozen stout arms were toiling at the wall. It fell bodily. The corpse, already greatly decayed and clotted with gore, stood erect before the eyes of the spectators. Upon its head, with red extended mouth and solitary eye of fire, sat the hideous beast whose craft had seduced me into murder, and whose informing voice had consigned me to the hangman. I had walled the monster up within the tomb!

1 Imagine you are the sub-editor of a large publishing business. Your boss has asked for a brief summary of the ending of *The Black Cat* to feature in a literary magazine. Decide what are the most important points of the extract above, and write the summary in exactly 50 words.

2 The language in the extract is quite different from that which is used by modern writers. Look for words and phrases that place the tale in the nineteenth century, and write down any examples you find.

3 Take a section from the extract and rewrite it for a modern audience. Then add a commentary to explain the changes you have made and why you made them.

Comparing Complete Short Stories

Read the two short stories which follow. The first is *Lucy Blue* by David Almond and the second is the whole of *The Black Cat* by Edgar Allan Poe. When you have read them make notes on what they have in common and what is different about them. You might consider some of the following:

- **Themes** – what are the two stories about? Are there links between the main plot lines?
- **Characters** – are the main characters similar or vastly different? Is the story personal to the narrator, or is it a third person account? What effect is achieved?
- **Setting** – the wider settings may be greatly contrasted, but are there similarities in the detailed descriptions of place? Think about why both may be set in houses.
- **Language** – David Almond is a modern-day writer from the north of England whilst Poe was an American writing before 1900. How does this affect the way each writes? Consider the impact of the different language styles – which is easier to understand? Why?
- **Action** – how well does each story evoke a sense of mystery, of uneasiness? How well is each story brought to life?
- **An unexpected twist** – do both tales have an unexpected twist? If so are they similar in any way?
- **What you are told and what is merely implied** – do they both build up atmosphere by gradually unfolding a story? Do you come to learn things without being explicitly told? Try and give examples from both texts.

....

Lucy Blue

I'd not seen Lucy Blue for years, and then the parcel came: the key to her house, the sharpened knife, the scribbled note: Key will let you in. Knife will end it. Please come to me. Set me free.

Lucy Blue. We were children together. We were little girls with short skirts tucked into our knickers splashing in the surf. She lived with her mother in a timber house way out on the headland. Beside them was the light-house whose light brilliantly swept the world at night. Beyond them was the cold Northumbrian sea, its chain of islands stretching to the horizon.

Her father was far away, and had been since she was born. She said he was a pirate chief swashbuckling his way across the hot seas of the south. When he sailed back he'd be laden with jewels and exotic fruits for us, he'd bring monkeys to play in the dunes and parrots to whistle in the pines. He'd take us away beyond the islands in his gorgeous sailing ship.

Sometimes as the dusk gathered and the lighthouse light began to spin, as I prepared to make my way back along the shore to my dull village, she'd grip me tight:

If you love me you'll believe me. It will be like that. You'll see.

She waited and the years passed. Her mother paint-ed the house as white as the lighthouse. She had cables laid from the village and switches and power points and dangling bulbs installed in every room. She laughed at Lucy:

We'll make sure he won't miss us when he comes sailing in!

And then at last he came, and we saw, and Lucy and I were chil-dren no longer. He was ragged and hunched, his face was black-ened with stubble and rage. There was cider in his pockets and slurred curses on his tongue. He reeled from his wife and drooled and smacked his lips for the pretty little thing he'd spawned.

And when I felt his gaze fall upon me I scurried homeward through the dunes.

In the village there were rumours of drug smuggling, and jail sentences in distant places. The people turned their backs to him. One day in The Angel there was a knife fight and one of the village boys was cut from cheek to chin. When they came to the headland at dusk to wreak revenge, the man's venom as he ran at them sent them fleeing as if from Hell.

I was forbidden to go there. At night I peered from my window. I watched the miles-long wedge of light sweeping the sea, the land, the sea again. As it passed, I squeezed my eyes against its glare. I tried to discern the glow of Lucy's house above the dunes. I prayed. I cried for her. I whispered to her, as if there were another cable linking her life to mine.

Lucy, I think of you still. Lucy, I love you still.

But more time passed, I felt myself growing away from her, my mind was drawn by other things.

And then we learned of the fate of her mother. She was lifted in a trawl net with her skull broken and with stones packed into the lining of her winter coat. Two detectives from Tyneside came to the village, went out to Lucy's place, returned without the father. They took lunch in The Angel and shrugged at all the questions. There was nothing on the man, they murmured. And they drove away.

After the funeral I went out there again. Lucy wore white like a bride and she told me that her mother had not really gone. She told me to stay until dark and see. All afternoon, I held her hand at the table.

Lucy, I whispered. Come back with me!

From deeper in the house came the muttering and cursing of her father, his snores, his whimperings, his calling from the depths of awful dreams. He lurched into the doorway at dusk, grunting some praise of the pretty girls of Bangkok and Ceylon.

Lucy, I whispered. Come back with me!

He staggered closer. I saw the knife shoved down inside his belt. I smelt his livid breath. His eyes reeled and his tongue rolled on his lips as he reached for me.

I ran home weeping through the swinging floods of light.

When I next went back I found her sitting on the shore. All around her were the scattered switches and power points and bulbs. Electric cables and wire were tangled in the heaped-up weed. She laughed and told me it was better this way. He'd ripped out everything. He'd said he couldn't bear to have light getting everywhere, exposing everything. She giggled, and held me, and drew me to the house. He was wrong, she said. It's the light that blocks everything. If I came inside and waited until dark, I'd truly see.

Inside were the scents of candles and burned paraffin. Again his whisperings and cries from further in. I held my friend, I gazed into her eyes.

Lucy, I whispered. Come back with me.

She smiled. We waited. I wept for the life that was being drained from her and she stroked my hand in order to comfort me.

Soon the lighthouse light began its pulse: long periods of dark and sudden bursts of light. I must just relax, she said. I must gaze about me in the room. I must allow myself to see. Outside, the darkness deepened. I imagined the long stretch of shore between me and my home. I trembled and she soothed me: it was all right, everything was all right. Wait until the light had passed and focus on the dark. The dark, each time a little darker. Soon I'd see.

There! she gasped. There!

She gripped me, nails biting my flesh.

There! You have to see her! There!

I stared across the table. The white flare of Lucy's face and dress plunged in and out of dark. Her eyes swivelled, she glared through me and past me and at me.

Oh, see! she begged me. Please see!

I heard him coming through the house.

Lucy! Please come back with me!

The door swung open and I ran.

And didn't stop running until I'd made a future for myself that was nothing to do with this place, and nothing to do with my friend.

And then, as if they had pursued me ever since that night: the key, the knife, the note: Key will let you in. Knife will end it. Please…
It was a day-long journey. I drove to the village, the dull place. I parked outside The Angel. I trudged through the dunes to the shore. The falling sun lit up the house and lighthouse way out on the headland. All along the beach were stinking heaps of weed and jellyfish, the endless line of waste thrown up by the sea. The sea itself was hardly moving, it was oily and flat, lazily slopping against itself where it met the shore. Not a soul to be seen. Closer in, I saw how Lucy's mother's paint had begun to peel away, how the timbers had distorted and cracked. Doors and windows were tight shut. I thought of calling but the words just gurgled in my throat. There were footprints in the sand, but leading everywhere, no way of learning anything from them.

Oh, Lucy! I prayed. Just come outside. Come back with me.

I turned the handle and went inside. The table as always. The candle and paraffin scents. The scent of the man: alcohol, bitterness and sweat. I stood in a corner of the room beside the door. The name I would cry still gurgled uselessly in my throat. From outside came the final screaming of the gulls as the light began to turn.

Lucy! I whispered. Where are you, Lucy?

But nothing, just time plunging onwards, intensifying the darkness, intensifying the light. I felt my tears running, heard the draughts in the timbers, the turning sea, something shuffling on the sand. I steeled myself, I gripped the handle of the knife, I stared into the dark, each time a little darker.

Lucy! Where are you, Lucy? I've come to see you, Lucy.

And then there she was, so sudden and so clear, in the opposite dark corner – the white bloom of her bridal dress, her smiling eyes in the white bloom of her face.

Oh, Lucy! I gasped, and I reached towards her. Come back with me, Lucy!

She disappeared in the pulse of light, reappeared in the stretch of dark.

Her lips opened and closed as if to welcome me but no sound came.

What is it, Lucy?

She drew back the collar of her dress, showed me the bruises and the lacerations, and then she smiled again, so joyous, and I began to see beside her the other woman, more obscure in her dark winter coat, and my heart leapt, and I said.

Oh, Lucy! I see! I truly see!

I moved towards them, but as I moved the light turned once more and showed me the man approaching on the beach.

I stepped back into the dark behind the door. I smiled across at my friend. I raised the sharpened knife. I waited for him to enter, this false pirate chief, this father, this fiend…

....

The Black Cat

For the most wild, yet most homely narrative which I am about to pen, I neither expect nor solicit belief. Mad indeed would I be to expect it, in a case where my very senses reject their own evidence. Yet, mad am I not – and very surely do I not dream. But to-morrow I die, and to-day I would unburthen my soul. My immediate purpose is to place before the world, plainly, succinctly, and without comment, a series of mere household events. In their consequences, these events have terrified – have tortured – have destroyed me. Yet I will not attempt to expound them. To me, they have presented little but Horror – to many they will seem less terrible than barroques. Hereafter, perhaps, some intellect may be found which will reduce my phantasm to the common-place – some intellect more calm, more logical, and far less excitable than my own, which will perceive, in the circumstances I detail with awe, nothing more than an ordinary succession of very natural causes and effects.

From my infancy I was noted for the docility and humanity of my disposition. My tenderness of heart was even so conspicuous as to make me the jest of my companions. I was especially fond of animals, and was indulged by my parents with a great variety of pets. With these I spent most of my time, and never was so happy as when feeding and caressing them. This peculiarity of character grew with my growth, and, in my manhood, I derived from it one of my principal sources of pleasure. To those who have cherished an affection for a faithful and sagacious dog, I need hardly be at the trouble of explaining the nature or the intensity of the gratification thus derivable. There is something in the unselfish and self-sacrificing love of a brute, which goes directly to the heart of him who has had frequent occasion to test the paltry friendship and gossamer fidelity of mere Man.

I married early, and was happy to find in my wife a disposition not uncongenial with my own. Observing my partiality for domestic pets, she lost no opportunity of procuring those of the most agreeable kind. We had birds, gold-fish, a fine dog, rabbits, a small monkey, and a cat.

This latter was a remarkably large and beautiful animal, entirely black, and sagacious to an astonishing degree. In speaking of his intelligence, my wife, who at heart was not a little tinctured with superstition, made frequent allusion to the ancient popular notion, which regarded all black cats as witches in disguise. Not that she was ever serious upon this point – and I mention the matter at all for no better reason than that it happens, just now, to be remembered.

Pluto – this was the cat's name – was my favourite pet and playmate. I alone fed him, and he attended me wherever I went about the house. It was even with difficulty that I could prevent him from following me through the streets.

Our friendship lasted, in this manner, for several years, during which my general temperament and character – through the instrumentality of the Fiend Intemperance – had (I blush to confess it) experienced a radical alteration for the worse. I grew, day by day, more moody, more irritable, more regardless of the feelings of others. I suffered myself to use intemperate language to my wife. At length, I even offered her personal violence. My pets, of course, were made to feel the change in my disposition. I not only neglected, but ill-used them. For Pluto, however, I still retained sufficient regard to restrain me from maltreating him, as I made no scruple of maltreating the rabbits, the monkey, or even the dog, when by accident, or through affection, they came in my way. But my disease grew upon me – for what disease is like Alcohol! – and at length even Pluto, who was now becoming old, and consequently somewhat peevish – even Pluto began to experience the effects of my ill temper.

One night, returning home, much intoxicated, from one of my haunts about town, I fancied that the cat avoided my presence. I seized him: when, in his fright at my violence, he inflicted a slight wound upon my hand with his teeth. The fury of a demon instantly possessed me. I know myself no longer. My original soul seemed, at once, to take its flight from my body; and a more than fiendish malevolence, gin-nurtured, thrilled every fibre of my frame. I took from my waistcoat-pocket a pen-knife, opened it, grasped the poor beast by the throat, and deliberately cut one of its eyes from the socket! I blush, I burn, I shudder, while I pen the damnable atrocity.

When reason returned with the morning – when I had slept off the fumes of the night's debauch – I experienced a sentiment half of horror, half of remorse, for the crime of which I had been guilty; but

it was, at best, a feeble and equivocal feeling, and the soul remained untouched. I again plunged into excess, and soon drowned in wine all memory of the deed.

In the meantime the cat slowly recovered. The socket of the lost eye presented, it is true, a frightful appearance, but he no longer appeared to suffer any pain. He went about the house as usual, but, as might be expected, fled in extreme terror at my approach. I had so much of my old heart left, as to be at first grieved by this evident dislike on the part of a creature which had once so loved me. But this feeling soon gave place to irritation. And then came, as if to my final and irrevocable overthrow, the spirit of PERVERSENESS. Of this spirit philosophy takes no account. Yet I am not more sure that my soul lives, than I am that perverseness is one of the primitive impulses of the human heart – one of the indivisible primary faculties, or sentiments, which give direction to the character of Man. Who has not, a hundred times, found himself committing a vile or a silly action, for no other reason than because he knows he should not? Have we not a perpetual inclination, in the teeth of our best judgment, to violate that which is Law, merely because we understand it to be such? This spirit of perverseness, I say, came to my final overthrow. It was this unfathomable longing of the soul to vex itself – to offer violence to its own nature - to do wrong for the wrong's sake only – that urged me to continue and finally to consummate the injury I had inflicted upon the unoffending brute. One morning, in cool blood, I slipped a noose about its neck and hung it to the limb of a tree; – hung it with the tears streaming from my eyes, and with the bitterest remorse at my heart; – hung it because I knew that it had loved me, and because I felt it had given me no reason of offense; – hung it because I knew that in so doing I was committing a sin – a deadly sin that would so jeopardize my immortal soul as to place it – if such a thing were possible – even beyond the reach of the infinite mercy of the Most Merciful and Most Terrible God.

On the night of the day on which this cruel deed was done, I was aroused from sleep by the cry of fire. The curtains of my bed were in flames. The whole house was blazing. It was with great difficulty that my wife, a servant, and myself, made our escape from the conflagration. The destruction was complete. My entire worldly wealth was swallowed up, and I resigned myself thenceforward to despair.

I am above the weakness of seeking to establish a sequence of cause and effect, between the disaster and the atrocity. But I am detailing a chain of fact – and wish not to leave even a possible link imperfect. On the day succeeding the fire, I visited the ruins. The walls, with one exception, had fallen in. This exception was found in a compartment wall, not very thick, which stood about the middle of the house, and against which had rested the head of my bed.

The plastering had here, in great measure, resisted the action of the fire – a fact which I attributed to its having been recently spread. About this wall a dense crowd were collected, and many persons seemed to be examining a particular portion of it with very minute and eager attention. The words 'strange!' 'singular!' and other similar expressions, excited my curiosity. I approached and saw, as if graven in bas relief upon the white surface, the figure of a gigantic cat. The impression was given with an accuracy truly marvellous. There was a rope about the animal's neck.

When I first beheld this apparition – for I could scarcely regard it as less – my wonder and my terror were extreme. But at length reflection came to my aid. The cat, I remembered, had been hung in a garden adjacent to the house. Upon the alarm of fire, this garden had been immediately filled by the crown – by some one of whom the animal must have been cut from the tree and thrown, through an open window, into my chamber. This had probably been done with the view of arousing me from sleep. The falling of other walls had compressed the victim of my cruelty into the substance of the freshly-spread plaster; the lime of which, with the flames, and the ammonia from the carcass, had then accomplished the portraiture as I saw it.

Although I thus readily accounted to my reason, if not altogether to my conscience, for the startling fact just detailed, it did not the less fail to make a deep impression upon my fancy. For months I could not rid myself of the phantasm of the cat; and, during this period, there came back into my spirit a half-sentiment that seemed, but was not, remorse. I went so far as to regret the loss of the animal, and to look about me, among the vile haunts which I now habitually frequented, for another pet of the same species, and of somewhat similar appearance, with which to supply its place.

One night as I sat, half stupefied, in a den of more than infamy, my attention was suddenly drawn to some black object, reposing upon the head of one of the immense hogsheads of Gin, or of Rum, which constituted the chief furniture of the apartment. I had been looking steadily at the top of this hogshead for some minutes, and what now caused me surprise was the fact that I had not sooner perceived the object thereupon. I approached it, and touched it with my hand. It was a black cat – a very large one – fully as large as Pluto, and closely resembling him in every respect but one. Pluto had not a white hair upon any portion of his body; but this cat had a large, although indefinite splotch of white, covering nearly the whole region of the breast.

Upon my touching him, he immediately arose, purred loudly, rubbed against my hand, and appeared delighted with my notice. This, then, was the very creature of which I was in search. I at once offered to purchase it of the landlord; but this person made no claim to it – had never seen it before.

I continued my caresses, and, when I prepared to go home, the animal evinced a disposition to accompany me. I permitted it to do so; occasionally stooping and patting it as I proceeded. When it reached the house it domesticated itself at once, and became immediately a great favorite with my wife.

For my own part, I soon found a dislike to it arising within me. This was just the reverse of what I had anticipated; but – I know not how or why it was – its evident fondness for myself rather disgusted and annoyed. By slow degrees, these feelings of disgust and annoyance rose into the bitterness of hatred. I avoided the creature; a certain sense of shame, and the remembrance of my former deed of cruelty, preventing me from physically abusing it. I did not, for some weeks, strike, or otherwise violently ill use it; but gradually – very gradually – I came to look upon it with unutterable loathing, and to flee silently from its odious presence, as from the breath of a pestilence.

What added, no doubt, to my hatred of the beast, was the discovery, on the morning after I brought it home, that, like Pluto, it also had been deprived of one of its eyes. This circumstance, however, only endeared it to my wife, who, as I have already said, possessed, in a high degree, that humanity of feeling which had once been my distinguishing trait, and the source of many of my simplest and purest pleasures.

With my aversion to this cat, however, its partiality for myself seemed to increase. It followed my footsteps with a pertinacity which it would be difficult to make the reader comprehend. Whenever I sat, it would crouch beneath my chair, or spring upon my knees, covering me with its loathsome caresses. If I arose to walk it would get between my feet and thus nearly throw me down, or, fastening its long and sharp claws in my dress, clamber, in this manner, to my breast. At such times, although I longed to destroy it with a blow, I was yet withheld from so doing, partly by a memory of my former crime, but chiefly – let me confess it at once – by absolute dread of the beast.

This dread was not exactly a dread of physical evil – and yet I should be at a loss how otherwise to define it. I am almost ashamed to own – yes, even in this felon's cell, I am almost ashamed to own – that the terror and horror with which the animal inspired me, had been heightened by one of the merest chimeras it would be possible to conceive. My wife had called my attention, more than once, to the character of the mark of white hair, of which I have spoken, and which constituted the sole visible difference between the strange beast and the one I had destroyed. The reader will remember that this mark, although large, had been originally very indefinite; but by slow degrees – degrees nearly imperceptible, and which for a long time my Reason struggled to reject as fanciful – it had, at length, assumed a rigorous distinctness of outline. It was now the

representation of an object that I shudder to name – and for this, above all, O loathed, and dreaded, and would have rid myself of the monster had I dared – it was now, I say, the image of a hideous – of a ghastly thing – of the GALLOWS! – oh, mournful and terrible engine of Horror and of Crime – of Agony and of Death!

And now was I indeed wretched beyond the wretchedness of mere Humanity. And a brute beast – whose fellow I had contemptuously destroyed – a brute beast to work out for me – for me a man, fashioned in the image of the High God – so much of insufferable wo! Alas! Neither by day nor by night knew I the blessing of Rest any more! During the former the creature left me no moment alone: and, in the latter, I started, hourly, from dreams of unutterable fear, to find the hot breath of the thing upon my face, and its vast weight – an incarnate Night-Mare that I had no power to shake off – incumbent eternally upon my heart!

Beneath the pressure of torments such as these, the feeble remnant of the good within me succumbed. Evil thoughts became my sole intimates – the darkest and most evil of thoughts. The moodiness of my usual temper increased to hatred of all things and of all mankind; while, from the sudden, frequent, and ungovernable outbursts of a fury to which I now blindly abandoned myself, my uncomplaining wife, alas! was the most usual and the most patient of sufferers.

One day she accompanied me, upon some household errand, into the cellar of the old building which our poverty compelled us to inhabit. The cat followed me down the steep stairs, and, nearly throwing me headlong, exasperated me to madness. Uplifting an axe, and forgetting, in my wrath, the childish dread which had hitherto stayed my hand, I aimed a blow at the animal which, of course, would have proved instantly fatal had it descended as I wished. But this blow was arrested by the hand of my wife. Goaded, by the interference, into a rage more than demonical, I withdrew my arm from her grasp and buried the axe in her brain. She fell dead upon the spot, without a groan.

This hideous murder accomplished, I set myself forthwith, and with entire deliberation, to the task of concealing the body. I knew that I could not remove it from the house, either by day or by night, without the risk of being observed by the neighbors. Many projects entered my mind. At one period I thought of cutting the corpse into minute fragments, and destroying them by fire. At another, I resolved to dig a grave for it in the well in the yard – about packing it in a box, as if merchandise, with the usual arrangements, and so getting a porter to take it from the house. Finally I hit upon what I considered a fat better expedient than either of these. I determined to wall it up in the cellar – as monks of the middle ages are recorded to have walled up their victims.

For a purpose such as this the cellar was well adapted. Its walls were loosely constructed, and had lately been plastered throughout with a rough plaster, which the dampness of the atmosphere had prevented from hardening. Moreover, in one of the walls was a projection, caused by a false chimney, or fireplace, that had been filled up, and made to resemble the rest of the cellar, I made no doubt that I could readily displace the bricks at this point, insert the corpse, and wall the whole up as before, so that no eye could detect anything suspicious.

And in this calculation I was not deceived. By means of a crowbar I easily dislodged the bricks, and, having carefully deposited the body against the inner wall, I propped it in that position, while, with little trouble, I re-laid the whole structure as it originally stood. Having procured mortar, sand, and hair, with every possible precaution, I prepared a plaster which could not be distinguished from the old, and with this I very carefully went over the new brickwork. When I had finished, I felt satisfied that all was right. The wall did not present the slightest appearance of having been disturbed. The rubbish on the floor was picked up with the minutest care. I looked around triumphantly, and said to myself – 'Here at least, then, my labor has not been in vain'.

My next step was to look for the beast which had been the cause of so much wretchedness; for I had, at length, firmly resolved to put it to death. Had I been able to meet with it, at the moment, there could have been no doubt of its fate; but it appeared that the crafty animal had been alarmed at the violence of my previous anger, and forebore to present itself in my present mood. It is impossible to describe, or to imagine, the deep, the blissful sense of relief which the absence of the detested creature occasioned in my bosom. It did not make its appearance during the night – and thus for one night at least, since its introduction into the house, I soundly and tranquilly slept; aye, slept even with the burden of murder upon my soul!

The second and the third day passed, and still my tormentor came not. Once again I breathed as a freeman. The monster, in terror, had fled the premises forever! I should behold it no more! My happiness was supreme! The guilt of my dark deed disturbed me but little. Some few inquiries had been made, but these had been readily answered. Even a search had been instituted – but of course nothing was to be discovered. I looked upon my future felicity as secured.

Upon the fourth day of the assassination, a party of the police came, very unexpectedly, into the house, and proceeded again to make rigorous investigation of the premises. Secure, however, in the inscrutability of my place of concealment, I felt no embarrassment whatever. The officers bade me accompany them in their search. They left no nook or corner unexplored. At length, for the third or fourth time, they descended into the cellar. I quivered not

in a muscle. My heart beat calmly as that of one who slumbers in innocence. I walked the cellar from end to end. I folded my arms upon my bosom, and roamed easily to and fro. The police were thoroughly satisfied and prepared to depart. The glee at my heart was too strong to be restrained. I burned to say if but one word, by way of triumph, and to render doubly sure their assurance of my guiltlessness.

'Gentlemen,' I said at last, as the party ascended the steps, 'I delight to have allayed your suspicions. I wish you all health, and a little more courtesy. By the bye, gentlemen, this – this is a very well constructed house'. (In the rabid desire to say something easily, I scarcely know what I uttered at all.) – 'I may say an excellently well constructed house. These walls – are you going, gentlemen? – these walls are solidly put together;' and here, through the mere frenzy of bravado, I rapped heavily, with a cane which I held in my hand, upon that very portion of the brick-work behind which stood the corpse of the wife of my bosom.

But may God shield and deliver me from the fangs of the Arch-Fiend! No sooner had the reverberation of my blows sunk into silence, than I was answered by a voice from within the tomb! – by a cry, at first muffled and broken, like the sobbing of a child, and then quickly swelling into one long, loud, and continuous scream, utterly anomalous and inhuman – a howl – a wailing shriek, half of horror and half of triumph, such as might have arisen only out of hell, conjointly from the throats of the damned in their agony and of the demons that exult in the damnation.

Of my own thoughts it is folly to speak. Swooning, I staggered to the opposite wall. For one instant the party upon the stair remained motionless, through extremity of terror and of awe. In the next, a dozen stout arms were toiling at the wall. It fell bodily. The corpse, already greatly decayed and clotted with gore, stood erect before the eyes of the spectators. Upon its head, with red extended mouth and solitary eye of fire, sat the hideous beast whose craft had seduced me into murder, and whose informing voice had consigned me to the hangman. I had walled the monster up within the tomb!

Drama

An A* candidate will be able to read between the lines of a text, recognizing and commenting upon subtext, motivation of character and structure. They will also read the text with subtlety, noting use of language and the effect and purpose of types of dialogue.

Study Skills

This unit will develop your understanding of the structure of the play, particularly focusing on characterization, dramatic device, symbolism and staging.

- **Exploring characterization** – this involves looking at a character's actions, dialogue with others, their movement, reaction to others, tone, and use and structure of language.
- **Learning about dramatic device** – this can relate specifically to character, for example their entrance at a particularly significant moment. It can be the timing of an event and how this relates to what has come before and what follows. It can also be the use of music which, for example, may be used to show a change in time period or that the present has become memory. A good example is the use of the flute in Arthur Miller's *Death of a Salesman*. A character moving from dialogue to monologue is relevant too. For a good example of this used as a dramatic device see the character of Iago in *Othello*. The use of lighting and the significance of props and stage also come into this category.

- **Distinguishing between different theatrical genres** – for example, Comedy, Farce, Melodrama, the Theatre of the Absurd.
- **Considering symbolism** – this is where signs or things are used to parallel or contrast the character in some way. Perhaps it is symbolic that a character who always speaks of escape continually looks out of a window though never opens it. A symbol can also indicate an important theme of the play.
- **Analysing staging** – it is important to think about the period in which the play is set as this will obviously affect the way in which you interpret the staging of the play. Staging relates to how the play is presented before an audience. How is the stage used? Are there different levels? How complicated are the directions in the play? Remember

89

that a play is meant to be performed so we must search through and analyse the instructions we are given in order to consider how it would work on stage.

Exploring Character

As an introduction to thinking about character, read the following extract from *A Doll's House* (1879) by Ibsen and answer the questions below.

....

A Doll's House

The Christmas tree is in the corner by the piano, stripped of its ornaments and with burned-down candle ends on its dishevelled branches. Nora's cloak and hat are lying on the sofa. She is alone in the room, walking about uneasily. She stops by the sofa and takes up her cloak.

Nora: (*drops the cloak*) Someone is coming now. (*Goes to the door and listens*) No – it is no one. Of course no one will come today, Christmas Day – nor tomorrow either. But perhaps – (*opens the door and looks out*) No, nothing in the letter box; it's quite empty. (*Comes forward*) What rubbish! Of course he can't be in earnest about it. Such a thing couldn't happen; it is impossible – I have three little children.

(*Enter the Nurse from the room on the left, carrying a big cardboard box.*)

Nurse At last. I have found the box with the fancy dress.

Nora Thanks; put it on the table.

Nurse: (*in doing so*) But it is very much in want of mending.

Nora: I should like to tear it into a hundred thousand pieces.

Nurse: What an idea! It can easily be put in order – just a little patience…

Nora: Yes. I will go and get Mrs Linde to come and help me with it.

Nurse: What, out again? In this horrible weather? You will catch cold, ma'am, and make yourself ill.

Nora: Well, worse than that might happen. How are the children?

Nurse: The poor little souls are playing with their Christmas presents, but –

Nora: Do they ask much for me?

Nurse: You see, they are so accustomed to having their mamma with them.

....

1   Looking at the first stage direction, what impression is created by the burned down candles on 'dishevelled branches'?
2   How is this symbolic of Nora's subsequent tension? In considering this, use language and sentence structure as evidence.
3   List Nora's actions before the Nurse enters. What impression is created of her character?
4   Contrast Nora's monologue at the beginning with her dialogue with the Nurse. Consider the significance, as a result, of her monologue and what purpose it serves as a dramatic device.
5   What change occurs in Nora when she speaks to the Nurse? How does Ibsen indicate that though she may have covered it over, her fear is bubbling just below the surface?
6   Nora has borrowed money from Krogstad. She has done this without the knowledge of her husband, knowing that he would not agree and, should he find out, would be extremely angry. Write the next section (the same length as this extract) where the Nurse leaves Nora alone. After a few minutes, Nora hears the door bell chime and believes it to be Krogstad. Begin with a stage direction.

Dramatic Device

Read the following extract from Arthur Miller's *Death of a Salesman*. Where dramatic device has been used there are numbers. Consider the purpose and effect of each and make a note of your ideas with numbers corresponding to those in the text.

Charley is Willy's neighbour and is concerned about him. He offers Willy a job but Willy cannot allow himself to think that he may need help and so is aggressive with Charley. Ben is Willy's deceased brother.

....

Death of a Salesman

Willy: I got a good job (**1**) (*slight pause*) What do you comin' here for?
Charley: You want me to go?
Willy: (**2**) (*after a pause, withering*): I can't understand it. He's going back to Texas again. What the hell is that?
Charley: He won't starve. None of them starve. Forget about him.
Willy: Then what have I got to remember?
Charley: You take it too hard. To hell with it. When a deposit bottle is broken you don't get your nickel back.
Willy: That's easy enough for you to say.
Charley: That ain't easy for me to say.
Willy: Did you see the ceiling I put up in the living room? …You gonna put up a ceiling?

Charley:	How could I put up a ceiling?
Willy:	Then what the hell are you bothering me for?
Charley:	You're insulted again.
Willy:	…You're disgusting
	(3) (*Uncle Ben, carrying a valise and an umbrella, enters the forestage from around the right corner of the house. He is a solid man, in his sixties, with a moustache and an authoritative air. He is utterly certain of his destiny* …(4) *he enters exactly as Willy speaks*)
Willy:	I'm getting awfully tired, Ben.
	(5) (*Ben's music is heard. Ben looks around at everything.*)
Charley:	…did you call me Ben?
	(6) (*Ben looks at his watch*)
Willy:	That's funny. For a second there you reminded me of my brother Ben.
Ben:	I only have a few minutes. (He strolls, inspecting the place.)
Charley:	You never heard from him again, heh? Since that time?
Willy:	Didn't Linda tell you? Couple of weeks ago we got a letter from his wife in Africa. He died.
Charley:	That so.
Ben:	**(7)** (*chuckling*) So this is Brooklyn, eh?

···

Activity

1   How are the two pauses used here? What do they add to our understanding of Willy?

2   What is the purpose of Ben in this extract? What does he represent?

3   What does Arthur Miller add to our understanding of the character of Willy by using Ben as a dramatic device?

4   Why is there '*Ben's music*' as well as the entrance of the actual character? What does this tell the audience?

5   What is the significance of Ben '*Looking at his watch*'?

Different Theatrical Genres

There are many different types of drama as well as different categories that we can place them into, dependent on the subject matter and structure.

Drama can be divided into theatrical genres, some of which are:

1   **The Theatre of the Absurd** – term applied to a group of playwrights working in the 1950s. They expressed through drama the belief that the universe was godless and held no meaning; all communication breaks down. As a result, logical and rational argument gives way to irrational and illogical speech.

2 **Comedy** – as opposed to tragedy – a play with a happy ending. Cynical comedies called black comedies became popular in the 1970s (for example Alan Ayckbourn). The dialogue is likely to be fast with quick exchanges between characters. Language is typically word play and use of puns.

3 **Farce** – a broad form of comedy involving stereotyped characters in complex even improbable situations. This differs from comedy in that the characters seem more extreme and less real. Ordinary situations are exaggerated to make them more of a parody based on types.

4 **Melodrama** – first applied to plays accompanied by music. The early melodramas used extravagant theatrical effects for artificially heightening emotions and actions, just as silent movies used music to tell audiences how to react. Acting was usually crude.

Read the following extracts and decide which categories they belong to.

· ·

1 **Danforth:** Mr Proctor, I must have good and legal proof that you–
Proctor: You are the high court, your word is good enough! Tell them I confessed myself; say Proctor broke his knees and wept like a woman; say what you will, but my name cannot–
Danforth: (*with suspicion*): It is the same, is it not? If I report it or you sign it?
Proctor: (*he knows it is insane*): No, it is not the same! What others say and what I sign to is not the same!
Danforth: …explain to me, Mr Proctor, why you will not let–
Proctor: (*with a cry of his soul*): Because it is my name! Because I cannot have another in my life! Because I lie and sign myself to lies! Because I am not worth the dust on the feet of them that hang! How may I live without my name? I have given you my soul; leave me with my name!
Danforth: …You will give me your honest confession in my hand, or I cannot keep you from the rope. (*Proctor does not reply*) Which way do you go, Mister?
(*His breast heaving, his eyes staring, Proctor tears the paper and crumples it, and he is weeping in fury*)
Danforth: Marshal!

· ·

2 Estragon, sitting on a low mound, is trying to take off his boot. He pulls at it with both hands, panting. He gives up, exhausted, rests, tries again. As before.

Enter Vladimir.

Estragon: (*giving up again*). Nothing to be done.

Vladimir: (*advancing with short, still strides, legs wide apart.*) I'm beginning to come round to that opinion. All my life I've tried to put it from me, saying, Vladimir, be reasonable, you haven't yet tried everything. And I resumed the struggle. (*He broods, musing on the struggle. Turning to Estragon.*) So there you are again.

Estragon: Am I?

Vladimir: I'm glad to see you back. I thought you were gone for ever.

Estragon: Me too.

Vladimir: Together again at last! We'll have to celebrate this. But how? (*He reflects.*) Get up till I embrace you.

Estragon: (*irritably*) Not now, not now.

Vladimir: (*hurt, coldly*) May one enquire where His Highness spent the night?

Estragon: In a ditch.

Vladimir: (*admiringly*) A ditch! Where?

Estragon: (*without gesture*) Over there.

Vladimir: And they didn't beat you?

Estragon: Beat me? Certainly they beat me.

Vladimir: The same lot as usual?

Estragon: The same? I don't know.

The first is an extract from *The Crucible* by Arthur Miller (1953). Proctor is told by Danforth to sign his name to a confession that states that certain women of the parish are involved with witchcraft. This would mean their execution. If he doesn't sign then it means his.

The second extract is from Samuel Beckett's *Waiting For Godot* (1952). The conversation between Estragon and Vladimir seems to have no meaning and lacks a clear purpose. It isn't progressing to reach an end, as a linear play would do, but has the motion of a circle. We would refer to it, therefore, as having a circular structure.

....

Activity

Write a comparison of the two extracts and, in doing so, answer the following questions:

* What is it about the language of the first extract that makes it dramatic in comparison with that of the second text?
* What do we learn of the characters in the second text? How are they different from each other?
* What is the difference in purpose between these two and how different do you think would be the experience of the audience in each case?

Symbolism

The following is an extract from *Doctor Faustus* by Marlowe. Doctor Faustus is ambitious. He believes that he has studied all that our society has to offer and desires greater knowledge, wealth and power. He decides to use a book of magic to summon up the Devil and make a bargain with him – Faustus' soul in return for limitless power and knowledge. The Good and Bad Angels have been used as a dramatic device but they are also symbolic.

Faustus: A sound magician is a demi-god!
Here tire, my brains, to get a deity!…

(Enter the Angel and the Spirit)

Good Angel: O Faustus, lay that damned book aside
And gaze not on it lest it tempt thy soul
And heap God's heavy wrath upon thy head.
Read, read the scriptures; that is blasphemy.

Bad Angel: Go forward, Faustus, in that famous art
Wherein all nature's treasury is contain'd:
Be thou on earth as Jove is in the sky,
Lord and commander of these elements.

Faustus: How am I glutted with conceit of this!
Shall I make spirits fetch me what I please,
Resolve me of all ambiguities,
Perform what desperate enterprise I will?
I'll have them fly to India for gold,
Ransack the ocean for orient pearl.

By using the device of the Good and Bad Angels, Marlowe is able to symbolize Faustus' dilemma and spiritual struggle. The Good Angel symbolizes his soul's place in heaven; if he practises magic and makes a pact with the Devil then his soul is damned. The Bad Angel is symbolic of Faustus' desire for wealth and power.

Compare the language of the two Angels: the Good Angel warns and the Bad Angel tempts. In externalizing Faustus' predicament, Marlowe is able to engage the audience in his struggle by showing us clearly the contrast between the temptation of one and the right path of the other.

1   What does the device of the Angels add to our understanding of the character of Faustus?
2   Analyse the language in this extract. What similarities do you note between Faustus and the Bad Angel? What is the significance of this?
3   What theatrical genre would you place this in and why?

Staging

Staging is when a director considers how to present a play to an audience. Often a playwright will include very specific directions for example, how the different levels of a house can be shown on stage, where windows are or how a room is set out. The time period that a play is set in will also affect the staging of it. Remember, everything is a clue as to the purpose and genre of the play.

1   Read the second extract below from *A Doll's House* and piece together what you think is happening. Imagine that you are auditioning for parts in this play; it is up to you to tell each character how to act in this scene, where they should stand and how they should relate to other characters. Make notes on each character with reference to the text and also write an outline of how this scene should look on stage including lighting, music, effects, and anything else you feel is relevant.

....

A Doll's House

Nora: There is no one has such good taste as you. And I do so want to look nice at fancy-dress ball. Torvald, couldn't you take me in hand and decide what I shall go as and what sort of dress I shall wear?

Hel: Aha! So my obstinate little woman is obliged to get someone to come to her rescue?

Nora: Yes, Torvald, I can't get along a bit without your help.

Hel: Very well, I will think it over; we shall manage to hit upon something.

Nora: That is nice of you. (*Goes to the Christmas tree. A short pause.*) How pretty the red flowers look! But tell me, was it really something very bad that this Krogstad was guilty of?

Hel: He forged someone's name. Have you any idea what that means?

Nora: Isn't it possible that he was driven to do it by necessity?

Hel: Yes; or, as in so many cases, by imprudence. I am not so heartless as to condemn a man altogether because of a single false step of that kind.

Nora: No, you wouldn't, would you, Torvald?

Hel: Many a man has been able to retrieve his character if he has openly confessed his fault and taken his punishment.

Nora: Punishment?

Hel: But Krogstad did nothing of that sort; he got himself out of it by a cunning trick, and that is why he has gone under altogether.

Nora: But do you think it would –

Hel: Just think how guilty a man like that has to lie and play the hypocrite with everyone, how he has to wear a mask in the presence of those near and dear to him, even before his own wife and children. And about the children – that is the most terrible part of it all, Nora.

Nora: How?

Hel: Because such an atmosphere of lies infects and poisons the whole life of a home. Each breath the children take in such a house is full of the germs of evil.

Nora: (*coming nearer him*) Are you sure of that?

Hel: My dear, I have often seen it in the course of my life as a lawyer. Almost everyone who has gone to the bad early in life has had a deceitful mother.

Nora: Why do you only say – mother?

Hel: It seems most commonly to be the mother's influence, though naturally a bad father's would have the same result. Every lawyer is familiar with the fact. This Krogstad, now, has been persistently poisoning his own children with lies and dissimulation; that is why I say he has lost all moral character. (*Holds out his hands to her*) That is why my sweet little Nora must promise me not to plead his cause. Give me your hand on it. Come, come, what is this? Give me your hand. There now, that's settled. I assure you it would be quite impossible for me to work with him; I literally feel physically ill when I am in the company of such people.

· ·

2   Write an act from a play about one of the following:

*   Four men/women who have spent most of their adult life in the army. They have just come out and are trying to be successful as civilians but finding it hard to adjust. Write what has changed for them.
*   A child that escapes their miserable life by pretending to be invisible. Sometimes their wish comes true. This should contain elements of reality that contrast strongly with the fantasy world they carefully create.

- Behind the scenes of a television station where life is chaotic. This should contain two main elements: the troubles and confusion off screen and the seeming calm that viewers see on screen.

For each of these utilize what you have learnt in this unit. You should think carefully and incorporate all of the five study skills mentioned at the beginning to ensure that you create something that is not superficial but has depth.

3   Write the first and final acts of a devised play where you concentrate on characterization and staging. Devised means that you base your play on source material but use your own ideas. Find out anything that you can about war. You could read Pat Barker's *Ghost Road* which is about life in the trenches. You should try to use as many different sources as possible so that your information is varied. You are looking out for information on the conditions soldiers had to suffer and endure.

- Read through all of the information thoroughly.
- Write down ideas that interest you or recurring themes.
- Now think in terms of a play structure.

You must create believable characters that contrast well with each other and include clear stage direction. Aim for originality.

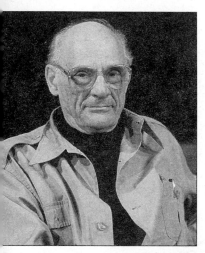

Arthur Miller

4   Working in pairs or in small groups, read a play from a period of your choice. It might be one of the plays mentioned in this unit (*Death of a Salesman, The Crucible, Waiting for Godot, A Doll's House, Doctor Faustus*). Take each of the four main areas mentioned in this unit: **characterization, dramatic device, symbolism** and **staging** and make notes whilst you are reading under these headings, including what genre you believe the play to be.

- Next write a critical response to the text using your notes as an aid. This is your title:

Analyse the play by commenting specifically on the playwright's characterization and staging. Consider any techniques employed, such as dramatic device and/or symbolism and conclude how successful they are in reflecting issues raised in the play.

The Novel

Studying a novel might at first be seen as intimidating. How do you study a large text? What are the relevant parts? What are you supposed to be looking for? What can a piece of prose tell you about the author, or the time in which it was written?

> A* candidates are expected to respond to texts in an original and critical manner. They must develop ideas with reference to structure and presentation. They will be able to make subtle comparisons within and between texts.

Study Skills

To accomplish these goals, you must work on certain skills, considering three main elements in the novel:
- Analysing character
- Appreciating setting
- Understanding language
- Using appropriate quotations showing textual evidence to back up your work
- Developing knowledge of the text as a whole
- Showing understanding of genres in literature

Tackling the Skills

This extract is from the introduction to *Dombey and Son* by Charles Dickens. The first chapter is of special importance in any novel, as it often introduces main characters, sets the tone of the novel, and creates certain expectations for the reader. Look at how the passage has been annotated with references to character, setting and language.

. . . .

Dombey and Son: The Arrival

Immediate introduction. Very impersonal

Oddly comforting description – care for new born. Comic effect

Specific time – one a replica of the other

Dombey sat in the corner of the darkened room in the great arm-chair by the bedside, and Son lay tucked up warm in a little basket bedstead, carefully disposed on a low settee immediately in front of the fire and close to it, as if his constitution were analogous to that of a muffin, and it was essential to toast him brown while he was very new.

Dombey was about eight and forty years of age. Son about eight and forty minutes. Dombey was rather bald, rather red, and though a handsome well-made man, too stern and pompous in appearance, to be prepossessing. Son was very bald, and very red, and though

Importance of name capitalized

Repetition of characteristics

99

*Time as human
personification.
Time and Care as
destroyers, ageing
and disabling man –
cutting him down*

*Comic irony. Actions
not like those of
exultation. A man
of little emotion*

*Reminder of time,
but also indication
of wealth*

*First thought is for
the house, not wife*

*Unusual description.
Dombey does not
see the beauty of
flowers, rather they
are mechanized,
business-like.*

(of course) an undeniably fine infant, somewhat crushed and spotty in his general effect, as yet. On the brow of Dombey, Time and his brother Care had set some marks, as on a tree that was to come down in good time – remorseless twins they are for striding through their human forests, notching as they go – while the countenance of Son was crossed with a thousand little creases, which the same deceitful Time would take delight in smoothing out and wearing away with the flat part of his scythe, as a preparation of the surface for his deeper operations.

Dombey, exulting in the long-looked-for event, jingled and jingled the heavy watch-chain that depended from below his trim blue coat, whereof the buttons sparkled phosphorescently in the feeble rays of the distant fire. Son, with his little fists curled up and clenched, seemed, in his feeble way, to be squaring at existence for having come upon him so unexpectedly.

'The house will once again, Mrs Dombey,' said Mr Dombey, 'be not only in name but in fact Dombey and Son; 'and he added, in a tone of luxurious satisfaction, with his eyes half-closed as if he were reading the name in a device of flowers, and inhaling their fragrance at the same time; 'Dom-bey and Son!'

*Fighting,
like a boxer*

*Dombey deals
in facts – a
business-like
view of life*

*Sounds self-
congratulatory.
He is proud to
have a son for
purely business
reasons*

Activity

1 Some of the highlighted words have been left without annotation. Look carefully at them and decide whether they tell you about
- Character
- Setting
- Choice of language
2 Comment on the effect of words like *darkened, feeble rays* and *distant fire.*
3 What does Dombey's *trim blue coat* tell you about the man? Consider the manner in which he speaks to his wife.

You can see just how much can be gleaned from the very first page of a novel. Already you know of Dombey's character, the setting in which the action takes place, and the comic effect of Dickens' language, whilst being conscious of a more serious message underneath.

Key term
Irony: a form of language by which a different meaning or purpose is present apart from the obvious, surface one. What is ironic about Dickens' portrayal of Mr Dombey?

Looking at Setting

The place in which the action of a novel is set is always important. It provides an appropriate backdrop to the plot and the characters. It can also add a particular atmosphere to the text.

In the following extract from Charlotte Brontë's *Jane Eyre*, the heroine has run away from her job as governess to the niece of Mr Rochester, a man with whom she has fallen in love. Feeling that her love will never be properly returned, she finds comfort in nature.

Jane Eyre: On the Heath

I touched the heath: it was dry, and yet warm with the heat of the summer day. I looked at the sky; it was pure: a kindly star twinkled just above the chasm ridge. The dew fell, but with a propitious softness; no breeze whispered. Nature seemed to me benign and good; I thought she loved me, outcast as I was; and I, who from man could anticipate only mistrust, rejection, insult, clung to her with filial fondness. To-night, at least, I would be her guest, as I was her child: my mother would lodge me without money and without price. I had one morsel of bread yet: the remnant of a roll I had bought in a town we had passed through at noon with a stray penny – my last coin. I saw ripe bilberries gleaming here and there, like jet beads in the heath: I gathered a handful, and ate them with the bread. My hunger, sharp before, was, if not satisfied, appeased by this hermit's meal. I said my evening prayers at its conclusion, and then chose my couch.

Beside the crag the heath was very deep: when I lay down my feet were buried in it; rising high on each side, it left only a narrow space for the night-air to invade. I folded my shawl double, and spread it over me for a coverlet; a low mossy swell was my pillow. Thus lodged, I was not, at least at the commencement of the night, cold.

Activity

Jane is comforted and cared for by nature. Charlotte Brontë carefully describes the way in which nature does this. She describes the setting, and creates atmosphere by using carefully chosen words.

Complete the table below, by finding in the text how each object is described, and then commenting on the effect of this description. The first two are done for you:

Object	Description	Effect
The heath	dry, warm with heat of summer's day	comforting, pleasant opening to scene
The sky	pure	clear, cloud-free, without problem— opposite to life with Rochester.
A star		
The dew		
The breeze		
Nature		
The bilberries		
Her hunger		
Her shawl		
The moss		

Activity

Jane awakes the next day before sunrise, cold and lonely. She lays huddled up until dawn breaks and the warming rays of the sun transform the pale morning.

1   Using this information, and what you learned about the setting from the previous extract, fill each blank in the following passage with the word you think is the most applicable.

2   Then compare the words you have chosen with those of a partner.

Jane Eyre: The Heat of the Day

What a still, hot, _____ day! What a _____ desert this spreading moor! Everywhere _____. I wished I could live in it and on it. I saw a lizard run over the _____ ; I saw a _____ busy among the sweet bilberries. I would fain at the moment have become a bee or _____, that I might have found fitting nutriment, permanent _____ here. But I was a _____ being, and had a human being's wants: I rose; I looked back at the bed I had left. _____ of the future, I wished but this – that my Maker had that night thought good to require my _____ of me while I slept; and that this _____ frame, absolved by death from further conflict with fate, had now but to decay quietly, and mingle in peace with the soil of this _____. Life, however, was yet in my possession, with all its requirements, and _____, and responsibilities. The burden must be carried; the want provided for; the _____ endured; the responsibility fulfilled. I set out.

Key term

This extract demonstrates **Pathetic Fallacy**, which means giving inanimate objects human emotions. In this context, then, it refers to the way in which nature seems to be in sympathy with Jane.

A Contrasting Setting

Look now at a short passage from George Orwell's *Nineteen Eighty-Four*, and notice how he creates a very different setting around his protagonist, Winston.

Nineteen Eighty-Four: The Room above the Shop

Winston looked round the shabby little room above Mr Charrington's shop. Beside the window the enormous bed was made up, with ragged blankets and a coverless bolster. The old-fashioned clock with the twelve hour face was ticking away on the mantelpiece. In the corner, on the gateleg table, the glass paper-weight which he had bought on his last visit gleamed softly out of the half-darkness.

In the fender was a battered tin oilstove, a saucepan, and two cups, provided by Mr Charrington. Winston lit the burner and set a pan of water to boil. He had brought an envelope full of Victory Coffee and some saccharine tablets. The clock's hands said seventeen-twenty: it was nineteen-twenty really. She was coming at nineteen-thirty.

Activity

1 From the following list, pick three words which best sum up the atmosphere evoked by the setting:

happy   contented   depressed   pessimistic   optimistic
cheerless   bright   gloomy   drearisome   tense   foreboding
plentiful   sufficient   cheerful   desolate   grey   melancholy
exciting

2 Just as you did with the first *Jane Eyre* extract, look at the following items from the Orwell text and note how they are described and the effect of this description.

Object	Description	Effect
The room		
The blankets		
The bolster		
The clock		
The oilstove		
The Victory Coffee		
The saccharine		

3 Write a comparison between the settings in *Jane Eyre* and *Nineteen Eighty-Four*. Use your completed tables to help you identify the differences in the way the settings are described.

Looking at Character

Below is the opening to *Moll Flanders* by Daniel Defoe. It was written in 1722 and many people consider it to be the first ever novel. Read it carefully, taking note of what sort of person Moll appears to be.

．．．

Moll Flanders

My True Name is so well known in the Records, or Registers at Newgate, and in the Old-Bailey, and there are some things of such Consequence still depending there, relating to my particular Conduct, that it is not to be expected I should set my Name, or the Account of my family to this Work; perhaps, after my Death it may be better known; at present it would not be proper, no, not tho' a general Pardon should be issued, even without Exceptions and reserve of Persons or Crimes.

It is enough to tell you, that as some of my worst Comrades, who are out of the Way of doing me Harm, having gone out of the World by the Steps and the String, as I often expected to go, knew me by the Name of Moll Flanders; so you may give me leave to speak of myself under that Name till I dare own who I have been, as well as who I am.

I have been told, that in one of our Neighbour Nations, whether it be in France, or where else, I know not, they have on Order from the King, that when any Criminal is condemn'd, either to Die, or to the Gallies, or to be Transported, if they leave any Children, as such are generally unprovided for, by the Poverty or Forfeiture of their Parents, so they are immediately taken into the Care of the Government, and put into an Hospital call'd the House of Orphans, where they are Bred up, Cloath'd, Fed, Taught, and when fit to go out, are plac'd out to Trades, or to Services, so as to be well able to provide for themselves by an honest industrious Behaviour.

Had this been the Custom in our Country, I had not been left a poor desolate Girl without Friends, without Cloaths, without Help or Helper in the World, as was my Fate; and by which, I was not only expos'd to very great Distresses, even before I was capable either of Understanding my Case, or how to Amend it, nor brought into a Course of Life, which was not only scandalous in itself, but which in its ordinary Course, tended to the swift Destruction both of Soul and Body.

But the Case was otherwise here; my Mother was convicted of Felony for a certain petty Theft, scarce worth naming, (viz.) Having an opportunity of borrowing three Pieces of fine Holland, of a certain Draper in Cheapside: The Circumstances are too long to repeat, and I have heard them related in so many Ways, that I can scarce be certain which is the right Account.

However it was, this they all agree in, that my Mother pleaded her Belly, and being found quick with Child, she was respited for about seven Months, in which time having brought me into the World, and being about again, she was call'd Down, as they term it, to her former Judgment, but obtain'd the Favour of being Transported to the Plantations, and left me about Half a Year old; and in bad Hands you may be sure.

....

Activity

1   Where are there records of Moll's real name kept?
2   Who are some of her worst Comrades, and what happened to them?
3   Why does she not want her real name known?
4   Based on these ideas, what sort of life do you suppose Moll has been leading in her later years?
5   How does Moll feel about crime? Which words lead you to your conclusions?
6   Who does Moll blame for the course her life has taken?
7   Do you think Moll is to be pitied, or is she trying to evoke sympathy in the reader which she little deserves? Which words help you to decide?

Daniel Defoe packs an amazing amount of information about Moll into just a few lines. You can see a depth to Moll Flanders' character within the first two pages of the novel.

Activity

Imagine you are one of Moll's comrades who has gone to visit her in jail. Write the scene of a play in which you have a conversation with her. Try to bring out the characteristics that she displays in the extract. Convey her personality without stating it too obviously, showing subtlety and originality in your work. Compare these two versions:

Moll: They caught me stealing bread from the baker's. Still they never found the watch I pick-pocketed from the man who arrested me.

Lily: Oh my, Moll. You're a woman of some resource – have you no shame?

Could be turned into this:

Moll: They caught me trying to save myself from starvation. I tell you, it was only a loaf to see me through to the next day. Still, the policeman's watch I borrowed from his pocket will fetch me a fair price when I get out of this place.

Lily: Oh my, Moll. You're a woman of resource – have you no shame?

In the second version, Moll's view of petty crime is highlighted by the excuse that she was very hungry, and that the pocket watch has simply been 'borrowed'.

Looking at Language over Time

Choice of vocabulary is important in conveying the right message to the reader. It is important both within a text (to describe characters and settings), and in comparing or contrasting two or more texts. An appreciation of why an author uses a particular word or phrase, and an ability to pick out and explain the important, information-giving parts of a text is what separates the A candidate from the A*.

Key terms

Moll Flanders tells her story by looking back on her life. In terms of the structure of a plot this is called **Flashback**. Other plots unfold in straight chronological order, whilst a few jump forwards in time, and then back to the main plot. This is called **Flashforward**. Some novels use two distinct plots and gradually draw them together. This is known as a **Dual Plot-line**. The opening to *Jaws* is a good example of this last type of plot.

Activity   First of all remind yourself of the key features of language across the centuries by referring to Literary Contexts (pages 147–159).

1   Below are a number of extracts taken from novels from the eighteenth, nineteenth, and twentieth centuries. They are jumbled up. Using clues in the language, group the extracts under the headings in the table below.

A   Soon after my return from Leyden, I was recommended by my good master Mr Bates, to be surgeon to the Swallow.

B   The hallway smelt of boiled cabbage and old rag mats. At one end of it a coloured poster, too large for display had been tacked to the wall.

C   I find that the district he named is in the extreme east of the country, just on the borders of three states, Transylvania, Moldavia, and Bukovina.

D   My wife and I knew Captain and Mrs Ashburnham as well as it was possible to know anybody, and yet, in another sense, we knew nothing at all about them.

E   As I walked through the wilderness of this world, I lighted on a certain place, where was a Den, and I laid me down in that place to sleep.

F   5 May – The Castle – The grey of the morning had passed and the sun is high over the distant horizon, which seems jagged, whether with trees or hills I know not, for it is so far off that big things and little are mixed.

G   It depicted simply an enormous face, more than a metre wide: the face of a man about forty-five, with a heavy black moustache and ruggedly handsome features… BIG BROTHER IS WATCHING YOU, the caption beneath it ran.

H   'And now,' she said, thinking that Lily's charm was her Chinese eyes, aslant in her white, puckered little face, but it would take a clever man to see it, 'and now stand up, and let me measure your lad,' for they might go to the Lighthouse after all, and she must see if the stocking did not need to be an inch or two longer in the leg.

I   I don't mean to say that we were not acquainted with many English people. Living, as we perforce lived, in Europe, and being, as we perforce were, leisured Americans, which is as much as to say that we were un-American, we were thrown very much into the society of the nicer English.

J   I looked and saw him open the Book, and read therein; and as he read, he wept and trembled; and not being able to contain, he brake out with a lamentable cry, saying, What shall I do?

K 'My dear, stand still,' she said, for in his jealousy, not liking to serve as a measuring block for the Lighthouse keeper's little boy, James fidgeted purposely; and if he did that, how could she see, was it too long, was it too short? She asked.

L In a little time I felt something alive moving on my left leg, which advancing gently bent forward over my breast, came almost up to my chin; when bending mine eyes downwards as much as I could, I perceived it to be a human creature not six inches high, with a bow and arrow in his hands, and a quiver at his back.

17th/18th Century	19th Century	20th Century
		K

2 Excerpts A–L come from six novels. Their titles are listed below. Looking carefully at the words used in these excerpts, identify the two that come from each novel.

1 *The Pilgrim's Progress*, John Bunyan (1678)

2 *The Good Soldier*, Ford Madox Ford (1915)

3 *Gulliver's Travels*, Jonathan Swift (1726)

4 *Dracula*, Bram Stoker (1897)

5 *Nineteen Eighty-Four*, George Orwell (1949)

6 *To The Lighthouse*, Virginia Woolf (1927)

Language and Imagery

You have already seen how language can be used to indicate the period in which a novel was written. Language is also important within a text too. Certain words carry particular meanings, for example yellow is traditionally associated with cowardice, and green with envy.

Activity

1 With a partner discuss what associations the following colours have.

Colour	Association
Yellow	fear, cowardice, or alternatively, heat, sun, warmth
Green	
Red	
White	
Black	
Purple	

2 Now read the following passage from *Tess of the D'Urbervilles* by Thomas Hardy. Written in 1891, it follows the story a young girl's first experiences of love, through to her final tragic actions against her seducer. In this extract from early in the novel, it is the May-Day festival, when all the women dance and process through the village. Pay attention to the colours and adjectives that Hardy uses and the way in which he creates a sense of fun but self-consciousness among the participants.

Tess of the D'Urbervilles

In addition to the white frock, every woman and girl carried in her right hand a peeled willow wand, and in her left a bunch of white flowers. The peeling of the former, and the selection of the latter, had been an operation of personal care.

There were a few middle-aged and even elderly women in the train, their silver-wiry hair and wrinkled faces, scourged by time and trouble, having almost a grotesque, certainly a pathetic, appearance in such a jaunty situation. In a true view, perhaps, there was more to be gathered and told of each anxious and experienced one, to whom the years were drawing nigh when she would say, 'I have no pleasure in them', than of her juvenile comrades. But let the elder be passed over here for those under whose bodices the life throbbed quick and warm.

The young girls formed, indeed, the majority of the band, and their heads of luxuriant hair reflected in the sunshine every tone of gold, and black, and brown. Some had beautiful eyes, others a beautiful nose, others a beautiful mouth and figure: few, if any, had all. A difficulty of arranging their lips in this crude exposure to public scrutiny, an inability to balance their heads, and to dissociate self-consciousness from their features, was apparent in them, and showed that they were genuine country girls, unaccustomed to many eyes.

And as each and all of them were warmed without by the sun, so each had a private little sun for her soul to bask in; some dream, some affection, some hobby, at least some remote and distant hope which, though perhaps starving to nothing, still lived on, as hopes will. Thus they were cheerful, and many of them merry.

They came round by The Pure Drop Inn, and were turning out of the high road to pass through a wicket-gate into the meadows, when one of the women said –

'The Lord-a-Lord! Why, Tess Durbeyfield, if there isn't thy father riding hwome in a carriage!'

A young member of the band turned her head at the exclamation. She was a fine and handsome girl – not handsomer than some others, possibly – but her mobile peony mouth and large innocent eyes added eloquence to colour and shape. She wore a red ribbon in her hair, and was the only one of the white company who could boast of such a pronounced adornment.

1   What is the significance of the women wearing white and carrying white flowers?

2   *But let the elder be passed over here for those under whose bodices the life throbbed quick and warm.* What impression does this line give of the younger girls in the procession? How do the colours mentioned in the description of them highlight this impression?

3   Which words highlight the girls' awkwardness at being in the public eye?

4   How is Tess set apart from the rest of the young girls?

5   What does Hardy tell us about Tess' character from her appearance?

6   What are the most important pieces of information in the passage? Which words and phrases would you be able to cut out from the text without losing any of the atmosphere? Try and edit the passage, to produce a re-drafted piece no more than 100 words in length. Remember how important language is to meaning, how symbolic particular colours are, and how descriptions of the girls highlight their youthfulness. Retain these key elements in your edited version.

Now read the following extract. It is the opening to *Last Orders* by a modern writer, Graham Swift. Think carefully about Swift's choice of language. Decide why it is different to most of the other extracts in this unit. Then answer the questions that follow.

••

Last Orders

It aint like your regular sort of day.

Bernie pulls me a pint and puts it in front of me. He looks at me, puzzled, with his loose, doggy face but he can tell I don't want no chit-chat. That's why I'm here, five minutes after opening, for a little silent pow-wow with a pint glass. He can see the black tie, though it's four days since the funeral. I hand him a fiver and he takes it to the till and brings back my change. He puts the coins, extra gently, eyeing me, on the bar beside my pint.

'Won't be the same, will it?' he says, shaking his head and looking a little way along the bar, like at unoccupied space. 'Won't be the same.'

I say, 'You aint seen the last of him yet.'

He says, 'You what?'

I sip the froth off my beer. 'I said you aint seen the last of him yet.'

He frowns, scratching his cheek, looking at me. 'Course, Ray,' he says and moves off down the bar.

I never meant to make no joke of it.

I suck an inch off my pint and light up a snout. There's maybe three or four other early-birds apart from me, and the place don't look its best. Chilly, a whiff of disinfectant, too much empty space. There's a shaft of sunlight coming in through the window, full of specks. Makes you think of church.

I sit there, watching the old clock, up behind the bar. Thos. Slattery, Clockmaker, Southwark. The bottles racked up like organ pipes.

••

Activity

1 Look at particular words and phrases in the passage:
   I don't want no chit-chat.
   He says, 'You what?'
   I never meant to make no joke of it and light up a snout.
   The way in which the central character, Ray, speaks is not Standard English; he speaks in the dialect of a particular region. Where do you suppose Ray is from?

2 Language in dialect is known as vernacular language. What effect does the use of a vernacular have in the passage?

3 Most novels are written in the past tense:
   Jack climbed the beanstalk.
   'You shall go to the ball,' said the fairy godmother.
   Which tense does Swift use? What is the effect of using this tense?

4 Many novels are written in the third person (he, she, it), allowing the author to show people's adventures. *Last Orders* is written in the first person (I), so that the reader sees events through the eyes of one of the characters.

• Ray is mourning the death of a friend. By getting us to look through his eyes, Swift conveys a sense of loss, of loneliness and of sadness. Pick out five phrases that create this feeling, and explain how they do so.

• How does reading a first person narrative feel different from a third person one?
   Which other extract in this unit is written in the first person?

5 Comparing *Last Orders* with *Tess of the D'Urbervilles*, which do you prefer? Give three reasons for your choice.

Looking at Genre

A genre is a style of any art form. For example in fine art, a painting might be in the genre of Cubism, Surrealism or Impressionism. In literature, genres include Romance, Crime, Fantasy, and Horror.

With a partner, write down as many different literature genres as you can think of in two minutes. Then write down the features that characterize each genre, and any book titles or authors you can think of who write in that style. For example:

Genre	Characteristics	Titles/Authors
Romance	Masculine hero saves beautiful but fragile heroine and they fall in love.	Mills and Boon Barbara Cartland

Science Fiction

One genre you have probably thought of is science fiction. This was first established in the form we know it today at the end of the nineteenth century by writers such as H.G. Wells (*The War of the Worlds*, 1898), and Jules Verne (*Twenty Thousand Leagues Under the Sea*, 1869). Since the Second World War, scientific developments have meant the introduction of robots, artificial intelligence, and atomic hand weapons into plots with futuristic settings.

Read the extract below from *Cal* by Isaac Asimov, and consider what you learn about the central character through the language.

Cal

I AM A ROBOT. My name is Cal. I have a registration number. It is CL-123X, but my master calls me Cal.

The X in my registration number means I am a special robot for my master. He asked for me and helped design me. He has a lot of money. He is a writer.

I am not a very complicated robot. My master doesn't want a complicated robot. He just wants someone to pick up after him, to run his printer, stack his disks, and things like that.

He says I don't give him any backtalk and just do what I am told. He says that is good.

He has people come in to help him, sometimes. They give him backtalk. Sometimes they do not do what they are told. He gets very angry and red in the face.

Then he tells me to do something and I do it. He says, thank goodness, you do as you are told.

Of course, I do as I am told. What else can I do? I want to make my master feel good. His mouth stretches and he calls that a smile. He pats me on the shoulder and says, Good. Cal. Good.

I like it when he says, Good. Cal. Good.

I say to my master, Thank you. You make me feel good too.

And he laughs. I like when he laughs because it means he feels good, but it is a queer sound. I do not understand how he makes it or why. I ask him and he says to me that he laughs when something is funny.

I ask him if what I said is funny.

He says, Yes it is.

••

Activity

1   Isaac Asimov manages to make Cal quite human in some respects, and this is achieved, in part, by the tone of the writing. What do you think the tone of this piece is? How do phrases like *My master calls me Cal; He just wants someone to pick up after him; I do as I am told. What else can I do?* help to create this tone?

2   Cal says that he is not a very complicated robot. How does the language convey this? You should consider the length of the sentences, the type of vocabulary used and the number of abbreviations.

3   In the extract below the opening to *Cal* has been changed to a third person narrative.
     IT IS A ROBOT. Its name is Cal. It has a registration number. It is CL-123X, but its master calls it Cal.

     The X in its registration number means it is a special robot for its master. He asked for it, and helped design it...

Describe the differences you find in the change of style, and the effect it has on the character of Cal.

Now read an excerpt from another science fiction tale by Isaac Asimov called *Kid Brother*.

••

Kid Brother

It was a great shock to me when our application for a second child was refused. We had really expected to get the licence.

I'm a respectable citizen; pillar of the community; all that kind of stuff. I was a little old, maybe. Josie – my wife – may have been past her best childbearing years. So what? We know other people worse off than us, older, trashy in character, who – Well, never mind.

We had one son, Charlie, and we really wanted another child. Boy or girl, it didn't matter. Of course, if there was something wrong with Charlie, if he developed some illness, maybe then we could license a second child. Or maybe not. And if we didn't get the licence, they would probably take care of Charlie as a defective. You know what I mean; I don't have to say it.

The trouble was we were late getting started, and that was Josie's fault. She had irregular periods and you never knew when to get her, if you know what I mean. And we couldn't get any medical help, either. How could we? The clinics said if we couldn't have children without help, that was great for the world. It's patriotic, or something, to be childless.

• •

Science Fiction, which is meant to stretch our imagination, is at its best when there is a thread of credibility running through it; when the fiction is not too far from the truth. In *Kid Brother* the contemporary issues of population control and childlessness are raised in a futuristic setting.

Activity

1   What do we learn indirectly about the world the narrator lives in?
2   What does the narrator really feel about children? Look at how he considers different ways of getting the licence.
3   How does he feel about his wife? Give textual evidence in your answer.
4   What might this suggest about the society in which the narrator lives?
5   Write a piece comparing and contrasting the two Asimov extracts. Draw on the ideas from your discussion of them so far. Your comparison should contain information on:
•   how the passages fit into the science fiction genre
•   the narrative voice
•   differences and similarities in character, setting, and language

Studying a Complete Novel

It is probable that at GCSE, and certainly at A-level, you will be required to read lengthy texts which may at first seem daunting and impenetrable. Below are some ideas to help you tackle the task of reading long novels.
•   Before reading the novel for study purposes, read it once in your leisure time for pure enjoyment.
•   Plan your first detailed reading of text.
•   Set aside time each day to read. Spend at least half an hour at a time, otherwise your reading becomes too fragmented and inefficient.
•   Keep a reading diary or journal that briefly follows the plot of the novel, but try not to simply retell the story.
•   Use bullet points in your journal to highlight key words about character and setting of plot (or annotate your own copy of the text).

- Make your reading active – draw doodles, diagrams and charts to help you remember important points.

Assignment

The following passage is a continuation of the opening excerpt from *Dombey and Son* on page 99. Paying particular attention to setting, character and language, make your own notes, and then answer the following question:

Through Dickens' use of language, what do we learn about Dombey's character?

....

Dombey and Son: Naming the Baby

The words had such a softening influence, that he appended a term of endearment to Mrs Dombey's name (though not without some hesitation, as being a man but little used to that form of address): and said, 'Mrs Dombey, my – my dear.'

A transient flush of faint surprise overspread the sick lady's face as she raised her eyes towards him.

'He will be christened Paul, my – Mrs Dombey – of course.'

She feebly echoed, 'Of course,' or rather expressed it by the motion of her lips, and closed her eyes again.

'His father's name, Mrs Dombey, and his grandfather's! I wish his grandfather were alive this day! There is some inconvenience in the necessity of writing Junior,' said Mr Dombey, making a fictitious autograph on his knee; 'but it is merely of private and personal complexion. It doesn't enter into the correspondence of the House. Its signature remains the same.' And again he said 'Dombey and Son,' in exactly the same tone as before.

Those three words conveyed the one idea of Mr Dombey's life. The earth was made for Dombey and Son to trade in, and the sun and moon were made to give them light. Rivers and seas were formed to float their ships; rainbows gave them promise of fair weather; winds blew for or against their enterprises; stars and planets circled in their orbits, to preserve inviolate a system of which they were the centre. Common abbreviations took new meanings in his eyes, and had sole reference to them. AD had no concern with Anno Domini, but stood for Anno Dombei – and Son.

He had risen, as his father before him, in the course of life and death, from Son to Dombey, and for nearly twenty years had been the sole representative of the Firm. Of those years he had been married, ten – married, as some said, to a lady with no heart to give him; whose happiness was in the past, and who was content to bind her broken spirit to the dutiful and meek endurance of the present. Such idle talk was little likely to reach the ears of Mr Dombey, whom it nearly concerned; and probably no one in the world would have received it with such utter incredulity as he, if it had reached him. Dombey and Son had often dealt in hides, but never in hearts. They left that fancy ware to boys and girls, and boarding-schools and book. Mr Dombey would have reasoned: That a matrimonial alliance with himself must, in the nature of things, be gratifying and honourable to any woman of common sense. That the hope of giving birth to a new partner in such a House, could not fail to awaken a glorious and stirring ambition in the breast of the least ambitious of her sex. That Mrs Dombey had entered on that social contract of matrimony: almost necessarily part of a genteel and wealthy station, even without reference to the perpetuation of family Firms: with her eyes fully open to the these advantages. That Mrs Dombey had had daily practical knowledge of his position in society. That Mrs Dombey had always sat at the head of his table, and done the honours of his house in a remarkably lady-like and becoming manner. That Mrs Dombey must have been happy. That she couldn't help it.

Or, at all events, with one drawback. Yes. That he would have allowed. With only one; but that one certainly involving much. With the drawback of hope deferred. That hope deferred, which, (as the Scripture very correctly tells us, Mr Dombey would have added in a patronising way; for his highest distinct idea even of Scripture, if examined, would have found to be, that as forming part of a general whole, of which Dombey and Son formed another part, it was therefore to be commended and upheld) maketh the heart sick. They had been married ten years, and until this present day on which Mr Dombey sat jingling and jingling his heavy gold watch-chain in the great arm-chair by the side of the bed, had had no issue.

– To speak of; none worth mentioning. There had been a girl some six years before, and the child, who had stolen into the chamber unobserved, was now crouching timidly, in a corner whence she could see her mother's face. But what was a girl to Dombey and Son! In the capital of the House's name and dignity, such a child was merely a piece of base coin that couldn't be invested – a bad Boy – nothing more.

Mr Dombey's cup of satisfaction was so full at this moment, however, that he felt he could afford a drop or two of its contents, even to sprinkle on the dust in the by-path of his little daughter.

So he said, 'Florence, you may go and look at your brother, if you like, I daresay. Don't touch him!'

The child glanced keenly at the blue coat and stiff white cravat, which, with a pair of creaking boots and a very loud ticking watch, embodied her father; but her eyes returned to her mother's face immediately, and she neither moved nor answered.

9

Poetry

In this unit you will be looking at how to analyse poetry. You may in the past have been asked to look at the language and organization of a poem, but have been unsure of what this means.

There are a number of elements that you must consider and comment upon with flair and originality in order to obtain an A* when analysing poetry. In this study skills section, we will define what these categories are and then go on to consider each of them in detail.

Study Skills

- Analysing the purpose and audience of individual poems
- Appreciating different tones
- Focusing on imagery and choice of vocabulary
- Understanding structure, rhyme, and rhythm
- Responding critically to individual and paired poems

Identifying Key Elements and Annotating a Poem

Read the poem below by W.H.Auden and the annotations that have been made. These were made in the light of reading the notes on key elements of a poem which follows.

A call, setting up intentions of the poem

Look, Stranger, at this Island Now

Direct and yet to unknown person – possibly the reader

Short line, closed, quiet

Look, stranger, at this island now
The leaping light for your delight discovers,
Stand stable here
And silent be,
That through the channels of the ear
May wander like a river
The swaying sound of the sea.

Multiple echoes of sound, alliteration, internal rhyme to create casual light-weight feeling

Onomatopeia – the sound of waves slapping into a hollow

Here at the small field's ending pause
Where the chalk wall falls to the foam, and its tall ledges
Oppose the pluck
And knock of the tide,
And the shingle scrambles after the suck-
ing surf, and the gull lodges
A moment on its sheer side.

Held at middle of word and pulled onto next line, like the shingle pulled

Alliteration, delicate images of boats on horizon

Rhyme to echo rocking momentum of waves and scenery

Far off like floating seeds the ships
Diverge on urgent voluntary errands;
And the full view
Indeed may enter
And move in memory as now these clouds do,
That pass the harbour mirror
And all the summer through the water saunter.

Internal rhyme, gently rocking, sending off to sleep, peaceful

Key Elements to Consider

- **Purpose:** What is the poet's intention in writing the poem? In considering this, look at the message of the poem, its main themes, its point of view and its perspective.
  Auden's purpose in writing this poem is to convey a sense of the sights and sounds of the island.
- **Audience:** Who is the poet writing for? Is it someone specific, or is it a more general audience?
  The stranger in Auden's poem could be the unknown reader; it applies to whoever is reading the poem.
- **Overall structure:** How has the poem been structured?
  Auden's poem is divided into three verses of equal length, but each line of each verse is a different length, so there is a contrast between the continuity between verses and diversity of line length within each verse. What effect does this overall structure have? Is it reminiscent of the wave and shingle movement as the tide goes in and out?
- **Tone:** What is the mood or atmosphere conveyed in the poem? How does it make you feel?
  Auden achieves a sense of calm and tranquility. The tone of a poem will be affected by the use of vocabulary, imagery, structure, and rhyme.

- **Vocabulary:** What type of words are used by the poet? Look to see if the poet uses simple, colloquial (familiar) or sophisticated vocabulary.
  Auden often uses words that sound like the thing they are describing (i.e. onomatopoeia).
- **Sentence Structure:** How are individual lines formed? You should look to see if the poet alters conventional word order and what effect this has. Look, too, at whether punctuation is used, and how it affects the expression of the poem.
  Auden separates the syllables of *suck-ing* on to two lines to resemble the shingle being pulled into the sea by the receding wave.
- **Imagery:** How does the poet paint pictures with words? You should pay attention to the images created and consider the significance of the images that are formed.
  Auden creates an image of sunlight dancing on the water very simply, but effectively with the leaping light.
- **Rhythm and Rhyme:** Do the words in the poem flow in a particular pattern? What is the effect of the rhythm in the poem? You should look at which syllables are stressed and which unstressed, if there is a rhyme scheme, and the effects of the rhyme.
  Auden subtly rhymes the third and fifth line of each verse to create a calmly repetitive effect like the motion of the sea.

Although it is important to be able to appreciate these different elements in poetry, it is crucial to remember that they are all interlinked and any skilled practical criticism will demonstrate this.

Looking at Purpose and Audience

Often poetry is written to be read by an unknown audience, and to be enjoyed as a beautiful piece of expression. Sometimes, however, poetry has a more specific purpose, and is directed to a much more obvious audience.

Read *Arms and the Boy* by Wilfred Owen, one of the foremost soldier poets of the First World War.

....

Arms and the Boy

Let the boy try along this bayonet-blade
How cold steel is, and keen with hunger of blood;
Blue, with all malice, like a madman's flash;
And thinly drawn with famishing for flesh.

Lend him to stroke these blind, blunt bullet-leads,
Which long to nuzzle in the hearts of lads;
Or give him cartridges whose fine zinc teeth
Are sharp with sharpness of grief and death.

For his teeth seem for laughing round an apple.
There lurk no claws behind his fingers supple;
And God will grow no talons at his heels,
Nor antlers through the thickness of his curls.

....

1   Looking at the first lines of each verse only, what impression do you get of war? Explain your answer.
2   Now look more closely. What is the intended effect of using a boy in the poem?
3   Explain the meaning of the line *Which long to nuzzle in the hearts of lads*. What is Owen really saying about war?
4   The first two lines of the third verse suggest the boy's innocence. Which words in particular help to achieve this?
5   Pick out all the words that are associated with death, danger, and evil. What is the effect of placing them alongside images of youthful naivety?

6 Behind the polite invitation made to the boy in the poem lies a sinister message from Owen. What do you suppose his purpose was in writing this poem, and who do you think he might have been writing for?

7 Using your ideas from the questions above, write a response to the statement:
In *Arms and the Boy*, Owen attempts to show us the effects of war upon the young.

Looking at Tone

Tone is concerned with the mood of a poem, and may be melancholic, light-hearted, comical or serious.

Read these poems by Seamus Heaney and Andrew Marvell. Both deal with a poet's love of a woman, but consider how different they are in tone.

The Otter

When you plunged
The light of Tuscany wavered
And swung through the pool
From top to bottom.

I loved your wet head and smashing crawl,
Your fine swimmer's back and shoulders
Surfacing and surfacing again
This year and every year since.

I sat dry-throated on the warm stones.
You were beyond me.
The mellowed clarities, the grape-deep air
Thinned and disappointed.

Thank God for the slow loadening,
When I hold you now
We are close and deep
As the atmosphere on water.

My two hands are plumbed water.
You are my palpable, lithe
Otter of memory
In the pool of the moment,

Turning to swim on your back,
Each silent, thigh-shaking kick

To His Coy Mistress

Had we but world enough, and time,
This coyness, lady, were no crime,
We would sit down and think which way
To walk and pass our long love's day.
Thou by the Indian Ganges' side
Should'st rubies find; I by the tide
Of Humber would complain. I would
Love you ten years before the Flood,
And you should, if you please, refuse
Till the conversion of the Jews.
My vegetable love would grow
Vaster than empires, and more slow;
An hundred years should go to praise
Thine eyes, and on thy forehead gaze,
Two hundred to adore each breast,
But thirty thousand to the rest;
An age at least to every part,
And the last age should show your heart.
For, Lady, you deserve this state,
Nor would I love at lower rate.

But at my back I always hear
Time's winged chariot hurrying near;
And yonder all before us lie
Deserts of vast eternity.
Thy beauty shall no more be found,
Nor, in thy marble vault, shall sound

Re-tilting the light,
Heaving the cool at your neck.

And suddenly you're out,
Back again, intent as ever,
Heavy and frisky in your freshened pelt,
Printing the stones.

Seamus Heaney (1939–)

My echoing song; then worms shall try
That long preserved virginity,
And your quaint honour turn to dust,
And into ashes all my lust:
The grave's a fine and private place,
But none, I think, do there embrace.

Now therefore, while the youthful hue
Sits on thy skin like morning dew,
And while thy willing soul transpires
At every pore with instant fires,
Now let us sport us while we may,
And now, like amorous birds of prey,
Rather at once our time devour
Than languish in his slow-chapt power.
Let us roll all our strength and all
Our sweetness up into one ball,
And tear our pleasures with rough strife
Through the iron gates of life.
Thus, though we cannot make our sun
Stand still, yet we will make him run.

Andrew Marvell (1621–1678)

....

Activity   1   Now complete the following table to help in the analysis of the contrasting tones of these poems.

Line	Poem	Meaning	Tone
When you plunged The light of Tuscany wavered	The Otter	memory of wife as animal causing light to ripple on water	meditative, calm
My vegetable love would grow Vaster than empires	To His Coy Mistress	sexual joke, double entendre– emotional/physical love would grow	teasing, suggestive
then worms shall try That long preserved virginity			
When I hold you now We are close and deep			
Now let us sport us while we may And now, like amorous birds of prey			
The grave's a fine and private place But none, I think, do there embrace			

Line	Poem	Meaning	Tone
You are my palpable, lithe Otter of memory			
I sat dry-throated on the warm stones. You were beyond me.			
And while thy willing soul transpires At every pore with instant fires			
And suddenly you're out, Back again, intent as ever			

2 Using the information from the table, write a short essay comparing the tone of the two poems above. Remember to use textual evidence to support your claims.

Purpose, Tone, and Audience

Activity

Read the following poem by Anne Stevenson and annotate it in the same way as the Auden poem on page 118. Then select lines that tell you something of the tone of the poem, who the intended audience is, and what the purpose might have been in writing it.

The Marriage

They will fit, she thinks,
but only if her backbone
cuts exactly into his rib cage,
and only if his knees
dock exactly under her knees
and all four
agree on a common angle.

All would be well
if only
they could face each other.

Even as it is
there are compensations
for having to meet
nose to neck
chest to scapula
groin to rump
when they sleep.
They look, at least
as if they were going
in the same direction.

Looking at Vocabulary and Imagery

It is obvious that vocabulary is what makes a poem; that without words there would be no poetry. But it is the poet's choice of words that relates the particular atmosphere or message to the reader, and it is important to appreciate how words work in a poem, and what effect they have.

Exaggerated Language

In Alexander Pope's *The Rape of the Lock* (1714), the story is told of a young, vain lady about to be presented at the royal court for the first time. Whilst there, a mischievous, merry young lord cuts off a lock of her hair. The humorous aim of the poem is achieved by Pope raising the status of the incident to epic proportions. Read this extract, looking particularly at the overblown language that Pope uses.

···

The Rape of the Lock: Belinda's Reaction

> Then flash'd the living lightning from her eyes,
> And screams of horror rend th' affrighted skies.
> Not louder shrieks to pitying heav'n are cast,
> When husbands, or when lap-dogs breathe their last;
> Or when rich China vessels, fall'n from high,
> In glittering dust and painted fragments lie!

···

Activity

1 What image is created by the words *living lightning* in the first line? What technical term is used to describe words that follow one another using the same initial letters or sounds?
2 Which words portray the horror of the incident? What does Pope say this causes more noise than?
3 Why is the fourth line particularly humorous?
4 The last image of a vase shattered into pieces suggests what about the whole incident as far as Belinda, the young lady, is concerned?

Pope works hard to choose words which will convey a sense of the atrocity committed upon Belinda, and her reaction to it, but which will also prove humorous in their exaggeration of the incident.

Underplayed Language

Images and tone are created by virtue of the type of vocabulary used. We have already seen how Pope uses grandiose language to exaggerate his tale, but other poets deliberately play down the language.

Read this extract from an earlier episode in *The Rape of the Lock* where Belinda is at her dressing table getting ready for her visit to court with the help of her maid.

....

The Rape of the Lock: The Dressing Table

And now, unveil'd the Toilet stands display'd,
Each silver Vase in mystic order laid.
First, rob'd in white, the Nymph intent adores,
With head uncover'd, the Cosmetic pow'rs.
A heavenly image in the glass appears,
To that she bends, to that her eyes she rears:
Th'inferior Priestess, at her alter's side,
Trembling begins the sacred rites of Pride.
Unnumber'd treasures ope at once, and here
The various off'rings of the world appear;
From each she nicely culls with curious toil,
And decks the Goddess with the glitt'ring spoil.
This casket India's glowing gems unlocks,
And all Arabia breathes from yonder box.
The Tortoise here and Elephant unite,
Transform'd to combs, the speckled and the white.

....

Activity

1   Notice the detail of the items on the dressing table, and the glorious luxuriance in which they are described. Who or what is being described in the following phrases:

- *The Nymph*
- *Th' inferior Priestess*
- *The Goddess*
- *The glitt'ring spoil*
- *All Arabia breathes from yonder box*
- *The Tortoise here and Elephant unite*

Now read *The Thorn* by William Wordsworth. In it he is as detailed in his description as Pope was in his, but consider carefully the language Wordsworth uses:

. . . .

The Thorn

There is a thorn; it looks so old,
In truth you'd find it hard to say,
How it could ever have been young,
It looks so old and grey.
Not higher than a two-years' child,
It stands erect this aged thorn;
No leaves it has, no thorny points;
It is a mass of knotted joints,
A wretched thing forlorn.
It stands erect, and like a stone
With lichens it is overgrown.

. . . .

2   From the list of adjectives below, pick out four which you think best describe the language of *The Thorn*.

> detailed   pedestrian   low   exciting   mundane   common
> simple   obtuse   confusing   luxurious   meaningful   easy
> clear   exaggerated   high   epic   folktale-like   sad

3   Using these last two extracts, write an essay comparing the language of *The Rape of the Lock* and *The Thorn*. To help you in your consideration of why the poets chose their particular styles, here are two pieces of historical and social information:

- Alexander Pope (born 1688), was plagued by severe illness as a boy, which stunted his growth considerably. He longed to be fully accepted at court, and whilst people admired his intelligence, he always felt that this would not happen because of his height.
- In his early life William Wordsworth lived in the rolling countryside of the Quantocks. In 1799 he moved to the Lake District and the countryside was to have a large effect on his poetry. Wordsworth made a deliberate attempt to write in a new, simple fashion for he saw himself not so much as a poet but as 'a man speaking to men'.

Looking at Structure

Structure in poetry can range from being very rigid to almost non-existent. Some structures define the type of poem, for example in the Sonnet, or in Haiku, whilst others lead the eye round into the shape of a star, or an animal. Structure, then, is not simply lines in an order; it actively contributes to the meaning of a poem.

Overall Structure

Look at the structure of the following poem by Edward Kamau Brathwaite.
It tells the tale of the poet performing the limbo. Putting the images that he
creates aside for a moment, consider how the structure of the poem mimics
the action of the limbo.

....

Limbo

And limbo stick is the silence in front of me
limbo

limbo
limbo like me
limbo
limbo like me

long dark night is the silence in front of me
limbo
limbo like me

stick hit sound
and the ship like it ready

limbo
limbo like me

long dark deck and the water surrounding me
long dark deck and the silence is over me

limbo
limbo like me

stick is the whip
and the dark deck is slavery

stick is the whip
and the dark deck is slavery

limbo
limbo like me

drum stick knock
and the darkness is over me

knees spread wide
and the water is hiding

limbo
limbo like me

knees spread wide
and the dark ground is under me

down
down
down

and the drummer is calling me

limbo
limbo like me

sun coming up
and the drummers are praising me

out of the dark
and the dumb gods are raising me

up
up
up

and the music is saving me
hot
slow
step
on the burning ground.

Activity

In analysing the structure of the poem you try to consider not just the limbo dance itself, but everything that surrounds that act:

• the rhythm of the music
• the time of day or night
• the way the limbo dancer must move under the bar
• the speed at which the limbo is completed

Look for evidence that the structure adds meaning to all these things.

Sentence Structure

Just as the overall structure is important in a poem, so is the internal sentence structure. Read *Words, Wide Night* by Carol Ann Duffy.

Words, Wide Night

Somewhere on the other side of this wide night
and the distance between us, I am thinking of you.
The room is turning slowly away from the moon.

This is pleasurable. Or shall I cross that out and say
it is sad? In one of the tenses I am singing
an impossible song of desire that you cannot hear.
La lala la. See? I close my eyes and imagine
the dark hills I would have to cross
to reach you. For I am in love with you and this

is what it is like or what it is like in words.

Carol Ann Duffy

1 The poet seems to be thinking out loud. How does the punctuation help to achieve this effect?

2 Where there is no punctuation at the end of a line, the sense and rhythm carry onto the next line – this is called enjambement. What is the effect of the enjambement?

3 Sometimes the punctuation forces you to stop in the middle of a line. Why do you think the writer does this?

4 The last line is separated from the rest of the poem, but connected to it because there is no full stop at the end of verse 3. Why might the poet have done this?

Assignment

Write a response to the poem below, *Island Man* by Grace Nichols. You should consider the following points:

• What the poem is about
• Who it is written for
• What tone is created
• What images are created
• Whether the lack of punctuation makes your understanding more difficult
• Why the poet is 'playing' with structure
• Whether there is a lack of order in the poem
• Which words are given emphasis and the significance of this

....

Island Man

Morning
and island man wakes up
to the sound of blue surf
in his head
the steady breaking and wombing

wild seabirds
and fisherman pushing out to sea
the sun surfacing defiantly

from the east
of his small emerald island
he always comes back   groggily groggily

Comes back to sands
of a grey metallic soar
                        to surge of wheels
to dull North Circular roar

muffling muffling

his crumpled pillow waves
island man heaves himself

Another London day

Looking at Rhyme and Rhythm

A sonnet is a poem with a very rigid rhyming and rhythmic pattern. There are three basic sonnet forms, one of which is the Shakespearian. It can be identified through the following features:

• There are always 14 lines
• There are always 10 syllables in each line
• The lines rhyme in this pattern – abab, cdcd, efef, gg

Activity

Using this information, fill in the blanks of this famous sonnet by William Shakespeare choosing words that seem appropriate to the sonnet pattern:

Sonnet XVIII

Shall I compare thee to a summer's day?
Thou art more _____ and more temperate.
_____ winds do shake the darling buds of _____
And summer's lease hath all too short a date.
Sometime too hot the eye of _____ shines,
And often is his _____ complexion _____;
And every fair from fair sometime declines,
By chance, or nature's changing course, untrimmed;
But thy _____ summer shall not fade,
Nor lose _____ of that fair thou ow'st
Nor shall Death brag thou wand'rest in his _____
When in eternal lines to time thou grow'st.
So long as men can _____ or eyes can _____,
So long lives this, and this gives life to thee.

Opposite is a poem called *The Identification* by Roger McGough. Read it through, considering the range of rhyme the poet has used. Note the idosyncratic use of apostrophes.

The Identification

So you think its Stephen?
Then I'd best make sure
Be on the safe side as it were.
Ah, theres been a mistake. The hair
you see, its black, now Stephens fair…
Whats that? The explosion?
Of course, burnt black. Silly of me.
I should have known. Then lets get on.

The face, is that a face I ask?
That mask of charred wood
blistered, scarred could
that have been a child's face?
The sweater, where intact, looks
in fact all too familiar.
But one must be sure.

The scout belt. Yes thats his.
I recognise the studs he hammered in
not a week ago. At the age
when boys get clothes-conscious
now you know. Its almost
certainly Stephen. But one must
be sure. Remove all trace of doubt.
Pull out every splinter of hope.

Pockets. Empty the pockets.
Handkerchief? Could be any schoolboy's.
Dirty enough. Cigarettes?
Oh this can't be Stephen.
I dont allow him to smoke you see.
He wouldn't disobey me. Not his father.
But thats his penknife. Thats his alright.
And thats his key on the keyring
Gran gave him just the other night.
Then this must be him.

I think I know what happened
… About the cigarettes.
No doubt he was minding them
for one of the older boys.
Yes thats it.
Thats him
Thats our Stephen.

Activity **1** Now complete this table to aid your analysis of the rhyme.

End of line rhymes	Mid-line rhymes	Effect
that mask of charred *wood* blistered scarred *could*		emphasizes the awful burns on the face; pulls us to the inevitable link from burnt wood to the child
	I dont allow him to smoke you *see*. He wouldn't disobey *me*.	embarrassed that cigarettes are found on his son; almost as if he tries to convince himself

2 The rhythm in the poem is like a one-sided conversation. What helps to achieve this effect?

3 Using the information from the table and your thoughts on how the rhythm works, write a response to the following statement:
The Rhyme and Rhythm in *The Identification* by Roger McGough makes the poem particularly sad and upsetting.

Bringing Poetry Alive

In the midst of all this close reading it is easy to forget that poems are not just for analysis; they are also for sharing, singing, and dramatizing.

Activity In groups of three or four produce a reading of a poem that will entertain the class.

1 First find and agree upon a challenging poem. Some suggestions for poets are as follows: Ted Hughes, Seamus Heaney, Sylvia Plath, Fleur Adcock, Anne Stevenson, Jo Shapcott, U.A. Fanthorpe, W.H. Auden, Lord Alfred Tennyson, William Blake.

Fleur Adcock

William Blake

Jo Shapcott

2 There are a number of ways in which you can tackle this activity:
- Act the poem out
- Use a narrator whilst the rest of the group take part
- Use music as a backdrop to your reading
- Repeat key words or lines
- Repeat a verse, as if it was the chorus to your poem
- Sing the poem

Try combining two or three of these suggestions, or better still make up some of your own. It does not matter what you decide as long as you enjoy experimenting with different interpretations of the poem.

Assignments

In this unit you have looked at each element of literary criticism in detail. In your assignment work, however, you will need to put all the pieces together into a coherent and comprehensive response.

1 Read *Follower* by Seamus Heaney, and decide which of the following themes are addressed in it: Nature, Childhood, Growing up, Family, Father, Being a poet, Death, Memories.

•••

Follower

My father worked with a horse-plough,
His shoulders globed like a full sail strung
Between the shafts and the furrow.
The horses strained at his clicking tongue.

An expert. He would set the wing
And fit the bright steel-pointed sock.
The sod rolled over without breaking.
And the headrig, with a single pluck

Of reins, the sweating team turned round
And back into the land. His eye
Narrowed and angled at the ground,
Mapping the furrow exactly.

I stumbled in his hob-nailed wake,
Fell sometimes on the polished sod;
Sometimes he rode me on his back
Dipping and rising to his plod.

I wanted to grow up and plough,
To close one eye, stiffen my arm.
All I ever did was follow
In his broad shadow round the farm.

I was a nuisance, tripping, falling,
Yapping always. But today
It is my father who keeps stumbling
Behind me, and will not go away.

•••

Now write a response to the following question:

Heaney thinks a lot about his father. How does this poem inform you about their relationship?

In your essay you should consider

- The themes of the poem
- The language Heaney uses
- The imagery he creates
- The rhythm of the poem
- The tone of the poem
- The structure of the poem

2   At GCSE level, you are expected to write about similarities and differences between poems; you are required to compare and contrast. Read the two poems below which deal with the same subject and write a response to the following essay title:

Compare and Contrast *A Description of a City Shower* and *Downpour.*

In your essay you should consider

- The themes of poem A and poem B
- The vocabulary of poem A compared to poem B
- The images both poems describe
- The differences in structure and punctuation
- The similarities in the tone of both poems

· ·

A Description of a City Shower

Careful observers may foretell the hour
(By sure prognostics) when to dread a show'r:
While rain depends, the pensive cat gives o'er
Her frolics, and pursues her tail no more.
Returning home at night, you'll find the sink
Strike your offended sense with double stink.
If you be wise, then go not far to dine,
You spend in coach-hire more than save in wine.
A coming show'r your shooting corns presage,
Old aches throb, your hollow tooth will rage.
Sauntering in coffee-house is Dullman seen;
He damns the climate, and complains of spleen.

Jonathan Swift (1667–1745)

· ·

Downpour

A strong rain falls, a bony downpour.
The waters roar, like a riddance.
The day vanishes suddenly
for fear of difficulties. The rain, for instance.

Through the letter box, leaves instead of letters,
Wet leaves blown along the path
and seeping through the low letter box,
an invasion that comes slowly,
but helped by rain. The downpour.

Penelope Shuttle (1947–)

10

Writing Skills

This unit identifies some of the writing skills you will need to gain top grades at GCSE English.

A* students should be able to do much more than write accurately. They show an ability to write in a variety of different styles – from formal examination answers to lively creative pieces; from journalism to leaflets. This involves developing a good ear for the way language works in different contexts: good writing usually depends on wide reading. Students should be familiar with the different styles used in different texts, and look at the structures and techniques used in each type. A* students are prepared to experiment. Their own writing is never dull.

Study Skills

- Writing in different styles in different genres
- Analysing passive versus active structures
- Using quotations most effectively in assignments
- Writing under examination pressure

Written Style

If you listen to a tape recording of someone you know, you will easily be able to identify their voice. Although we speak the same language, we have distinctive ways of speaking. Linguists call this an idiolect – the individual way each of us speaks.

The same applies to writing. As we become more skilful writers, we develop our own written style. But the key to success at GCSE and beyond is being able to adapt your written style to different purposes and audiences. A letter of complaint to a supermarket needs a different style from a story about an alien attack; a factual leaflet needs a different style from a personal diary, for example. The most skilful writers adopt the style which feels perfectly suited to their purpose and audience. This will be explored further in the unit.

Plain English

Writers usually use language to communicate their thoughts, feelings, and ideas clearly. However, it can sometimes seem as if language is being used to confuse the reader, or to prevent us from knowing something. This section looks at plain English … and its enemies.

1   This paragraph appeared in a school publication. How would you summarize its meaning in one sentence?:

> Totally obsolete teaching methods based on imprinting concepts instead of growthful actualizing of potential have created the intellectual ghetto. If schools would stop labelling co-operation 'cheating' and adopt newer methods of student interaction, we wouldn't keep churning out these competitive isolates.

Language becomes dense and tangled in this way when the vocabulary is chosen to impress rather than to inform. The writer goes for the complex word rather than the straightforward one:

> The problem is how to optimize the institutionalization of the forecasting procedures.

2   See how far you can take this misuse of vocabulary. Take a well-known story such as *Little Red Riding Hood* and use a thesaurus to explore the effect of using words chosen to impress rather than communicate directly. Write a 'translation' underneath. You might start like this:

> A considerable temporal space prior to the present, a relatively unfledged female commonly referred to by the appellation of Little Red Riding Hood (on account of her distinctive accoutrements) determined that she would perambulate through the arboriculture in the vicinity of her grandmother's homestead…

> **Translation**
> Once upon a time a young girl called Little Red Riding Hood (becuse of the clothes she wore) decided to walk in the woods near her grandmother's house…

Impersonal Style

Some forms of writing demand an impersonal written style, one where the personality of the writer is kept in the background. Legal documents are an obvious example of this.

One key grammatical structure used in these documents is the passive voice. This enables a writer to hide the main subject of a sentence. Here are some examples:

Active version	Passive version
Lord Morris built the house in 1867.	The house was built in 1867.
We burned the magnesium in the flame.	Magnesium was burned in the the flame.
You need hops to make beer.	Hops are needed to make beer.
The Chancellor announced yesterday that the Government is in severe debt.	It was announced yesterday that the Government is in severe debt.

Passive structures can be useful for making a text less personal. In science, for example, it is often the process that matters, rather than who performed it. But passives can also be used to conceal the truth, as in that last example. The passive version will always make the astute reader pose questions: Who actually did the announcing? An official of the Government? A Minister? Or was the information leaked? For this reason, the passive is often a useful tool for lawyers, politicians, and journalists.

Lack of Clarity

Writing can also lack clarity when it is not properly controlled.

Activity

Compare these two examples. One is a letter from a shopkeeper in York. The second is a council letter about housing rents.

1   What makes the two letters poor examples of clear communication?
2   How would you improve the clarity of either of these texts – paying attention to the vocabulary and structure? Choose one text and rewrite it in plain English.
3   Now write a brief commentary explaining the main changes that you have made.

Shops suffering

Much as the tourism initiative is to be welcomed (July 27), it must also be aimed at the surrounding areas to get people in from a 50 mile radius round York to come and shop and not only inside the city wall but also the other shopping areas such as Bishopthorpe Road, Acomb, Heworth, etc.

It is not only shops inside the city walls that are suffering, most of us have the same problems outside as well. The introduction of resident only parking has greatly affected our business, and it must be said that considerable relaxation in the operation of these schemes is possible, the allowing of parking one hour or longer between 9.30am and 4.30 am would greatly assist the survival of many small businesses. People from outlying areas are regularly telling us we hate having to come to York the parking is terrible and expensive, and we only come if we have to, and there is your answer. I have said it before and I will say it again, trade or die.

I have read in your columns before that people no longer find the shops which are a bit different in York city centre (I have no doubt older readers will remember these shops as I do) when visiting. If they tour round the areas already mentioned they will find some of these interesting shops forced out by silly rents, etc, a legacy of the property boom of past years.

How long they will survive now depends on the will of the local council to help them stay in business?

B. Rollinson
Acomb
York

Dear Sir/Madam

I am writing to inform you that the City Council at their meeting on 25th July 1979, in accordance with the duty imposed by section 113(1A) of the Housing Act, 1957, to review rents from time to time and to make such changes, either of the rents generally or of particular rents, as circumstances may require, decided that the net rents (ie exclusive of rates) of all Council-owned dwellings should continue to be related to Gross Rateable Values and adopted a general basis of 130% of Gross Rateable value as the level at which the net rents should be set …

Using Quotations

We use quotations to support the points we are making in a piece of critical writing. A coursework or examination literature assignment without quotations is unlikely to gain higher than Grade C. Equally, it is possible to use too many quotations, or to use quotations that are too long.

Activity

Read the extracts below from literature assignments by a number of Year 10 students. Look at the way their use of quotations contributes to the overall effect – a poor use of quotations weakens the style and argument of the answer.

1 Working on your own or with a partner, decide for each one:
- Whether quotations are: underused, about the right level of use, excessively used
- What the effect is, for example: points seem unsupported by quotation; the text feels clogged with quotation; the text is fluent and easy to read
- What advice you could give to improve each answer
- The order the answers should be in from best to worst.

Answer A

The author of *I Used to Live Here Once* suggests the familiarity with the scenes she describes by showing that the narrator remembers each detail of the island, *'remembering each one'*. She could always remember each stepping stone, *'she remembered the stepping stone'*. And the steps that were leading up to the house, *'the steps led up to the house'*.

Vicky

Answer B

Before Macbeth meets the witches we learn that he has just fought a fierce battle. In it he has defeated the king's rivals and helped to save Scotland. We learn from the account of the battle that Macbeth has been brutally brave, earning the admiration of all around him. He is rewarded with the title Thane of Cawdor, and this is the point at which his dark ambitions begin to take him over.

John

Answer C

Up to this point in the play Brutus has for the most part appeared measured and intelligent, as well as being highly respected by his fellow Romans. Whereas Cassius was motivated to kill Caesar principally for personal gain (and the other conspirators likewise) Brutus seemed honestly to believe that it was done for the good of Rome. This view is indicated in the soliloquy of Act 2, scene 1 lines 10–34 in which he had only himself to fool.

Tim

Answer D

Thomas Hardy's *Tess of the d'Urbervilles* shows a *'pure woman'* doomed to a life of betrayal, despair and depondency. Her own family are the first culprits in her downfall. When both parents are successfully wooed by the *'humorousness and jollity'* of the Pure Drop Inn, it is left to Tess to go to the inn where a *'reproachful flash'* from her dark eyes is all that it takes to return her now sheepish parents to their rightful abode.

Laura

Answer E

Dr Frankenstein uses aggressive language when he speaks to the monster: *'Abhorred monster! Fiend that thou art! The tortures of hell are too mild a vengeance for thy crimes. Wretched devil'* In comparison the monster seems intelligent and restrained: *'I expected this reception,'* said the demon. *'All men hate the wretched; how then must I be hated who am miserable beyond all living things!'*
The monster also complains about his treatment:
'How dare you sport thus with life? Do your duty towards me…'
We feel some sympathy for the monster:
'If you will comply with my conditions, I will leave them and you at peace.'

Sarah

2 Now compare your responses to Answers A–E with these from a GCSE examiner:

A *The strength of this is that it refers closely to the text. But the effect is spoilt because the quotations are so poorly integrated. They just repeat – almost word for word – what the student has already said. They feel tagged-on and messy.*

B *This shows a sound understanding of the text. There is some promising vocabulary. But it could not achieve higher than a C grade because points are not supported by quotations.*

C *This feels like an impressive answer – the expression is certainly high level. But it lacks direct quotations. The reference to a scene is not enough – we need to see the exact words the student is referring to.*

D   *This is a skilful answer, with a really accomplished balance of personal response and quotation. The quotations are well integrated into the student's style so that they help move the argument along, rather than slow it down. This is a what an A* use of quotations feels like.*

E   *This is a typical answer from someone who knows that s/he has to use quotations. She uses them in blocks, breaking up her essay and making it very unsatisfying to read. Quotations should be integrated into your style, rather than placed in blocks like this. If you do quote more than a sentence at a time, you should refer back to it in detail in the following paragraph.*

The examiner's ranking of these answers is as follows:
B (worst – no supporting quotations; plodding style: Grade C)
A
E
C
D (skilfully integrated quotations; fluent, mature style: Grade A*)

Checklist for using quotations:
- Use quotations to support each point
- Keep quotations brief – preferably to just two or three words embedded in your own sentence
- For quotations of more than a sentence, place them in a separate paragraph
- When using longer quotations (i.e. a sentence or more), aim to refer back to the quotation, giving your views about the language or technique the writer has used.

Writing Under Timed Conditions

Some students excel at coursework assignments. They enjoy the process of brainstorming ideas, drafting, redrafting, polishing, and then submitting a final version. But this is a luxury you will not have in the final examinations. Up to 70% of your final marks will be based on what you can produce under the of pressure timed conditions.
The following pages contain suggestions for improving your writing in exam conditions.

1 Practice

You need to get as much practice as possible of working in timed conditions. In the last two or three months of your English course, aim to produce at least one timed assignment every fortnight. In this way, you will get used to the feeling of working under pressure and, although the exams may still feel stressful, you will have proved to yourself that you can cope.

2 Plan

Successful students always take the first few minutes of the time allotted to plan an answer.

Look closely at the question. Be active: underline, highlight, circle key words. Do not just answer the question you had hoped would be asked – make sure you're answering the exact question.

Write down as many thoughts and ideas as possible, and then begin to order them. Most timed essays take up between 5 and 8 paragraphs, so once you have your main ideas together, number the points to give them a logical sequence.

3 Be lively

Remember that examiners mark hundreds of examination scripts at a time. Most of the scripts will seem very similiar. So make yours different. Grab the examiner's attention.

Use topic sentences at the start of paragraphs to show what the paragraph is about.

Place short sentences next to long sentences to create an interesting rhythm and pace.

Do not make your vocabulary flowery – instead keep it visual and precise. Choose words which lead the examiner into the world of your essay, helping them grasp exactly what you are saying.

Be adventurous with creative writing: use a variety of dialogue, description and storytelling. Cut from one narrative to a second storyline if appropriate.

In literature assignments, give your response and then support it with evidence from the text.

4 Be accurate

You could probably achieve a top grade without being perfectly accurate – but why settle for less? Leave yourself time to read through your answers. Check them through to ensure they make sense.

Are there parts that feel garbled and confused, or paragraphs that need clearer linking phrases (like *on the other hand ... although ... however*)? Are there fancy words which would be more effective if replaced with simpler more direct vocabulary?

Does your use of punctuation help the reader to follow your meaning? Are you using commas to separate ideas and words in a list; semi-colons to create balance within sentences; colons to hint at something coming up; full stops to show the boundaries between sentences?

5 Keep reading

Reading widely is at the heart of success in English. If you enjoy getting to grips with a range of texts, you will usually be more effective in writing in a range of styles. Read magazines. Choose short stories by an author you have never heard of. Listen to the language of news broadcasts. Pick up leaflets in the doctor's waiting room. Devour different types of texts. All of these sources will help you to get a sharper feel for the way texts work and, in turn, to write more successfully in a range of styles and for a variety of audiences.

Biography pages

Literature becomes more interesting as you learn about the writers and their lives and times. This section gives just a flavour of the background to some of the writers featured in *Top Grade English*.

Daniel Defoe (1660–1731)

Defoe is one of the most colourful characters in English literature. He was born in London, the son of a butcher. In his early life he was a hosiery merchant, selling stockings, and at the same time writing political pamphlets. This was an age when people enjoyed heated debates promoted by spoof documents. For example, Defoe wrote an essay attacking people who questioned the Church of England … even though he himself questioned the Church of England. As a result he spent six months in prison. During his lifetime he wrote 560 books and pamphlets, and is best known for *Robinson Crusoe* (based on a true story of a shipwrecked sailor) and *Moll Flanders*.

What was significant about his work and why has it lasted? Chiefly because he created memorable characters, like Moll Flanders, who were ordinary people, often with vices and unpleasant habits, who struggle to survive. His characters feel deeply human – and, almost 300 years later, we still see in them something we can understand. *(See p. 104)*

Edgar Allan Poe (1809–49)

Edgar Allan Poe is sometimes described as the inventor of modern horror fiction. He certainly created some fairly haunting stories – people killing other people, being tortured, imagining their own deaths. He had a powerful influence on the modern detective story, especially with his *Murders in the Rue Morgue*, which keeps the reader guessing. Poe had a miserable life – an unhappy childhood, then poverty, a nervous disorder and alcoholism, and his work for many readers has a disturbing, unsettling effect. *(See p. 75)*

Charlotte Brontë (1816–55)

Charlotte lived with her four sisters and one brother in Haworth, a bleak and windswept spot on the Yorkshire Moors, in the heart of the Aire Valley – famous last century for its high mortality rate from the disease consumption. Cut off from civilization, the children created a fantasy world, which led to an astonishing outpouring of writing from Anne, Emily and Charlotte. Charlotte's work was the most conventional – straightforward narratives following a main character. Emily's were darker, more troubled and confusing. Like her sisters, Charlotte had to hide her identity as a woman initially in order to get her books accepted. Her most famous work is undoubtedly *Jane Eyre* which, in the style of the period, follows the fortune of an orphaned child to her final happiness in marriage. *(See p. 101)*

Charles Dickens (1812–70)

Perhaps the most famous writer of the nineteenth century, Dickens wrote unstoppably, setting himself and meeting apparently impossible deadlines. His early novels, for example *Nicholas Nickleby* were sunny comedies, with layers of melodrama; his later works darkened and tackled more sober themes (for example, the theme of debt in *Bleak House*). He established magazines, wrote Christmas stories, gave three-hour readings to an adoring public. As one critic says: 'So prolific is his output and so frenzied his life, it seems miraculous he lived as long as he did' (Ian Ousby). *(See p. 99)*

Henrik Ibsen (1828–1906)

This Norwegian playwright is usually seen as the creator of modern drama and, in many respects, he established the pattern for the modern-day soap opera. His work is usually realistic: he showed real people in real situations, something which hadn't happened before. Drama of the period was dominated by melodrama – two-dimensional characters in predictable or far-fetched situations. Ibsen shocked society by showing a woman in a loveless marriage who walked out, slamming the door behind her; or showing the damaging effects of venereal disease on a respectable household. Critics were appalled and audiences walked out. But drama could never quite be the same again – and the way was paved for the theatre to reflect the genuine concerns of people, in the way that soap operas continue to do. *(See p. 90)*

Doris Lessing (1919–)

Doris Lessing is known for several main strands of writing: stories and novels which are science fiction; other stories; autobiography and travel writing. Her early novel *The Grass is Singing* shows a world ripped apart when a taboo is broken: a white woman in South Africa (where apartheid prevailed until recently) has a relationship with her black servant. Equally disturbing is her much later novel, *The Fifth Child*, in which a deviant child wreaks havoc first on his family, then on the local community. Lessing's work is sometimes realistic, sometimes experimental. *(See p. 12)*

Alexander Pope (1688–1744)

Pope's Health was damaged in childhood by tuberculosis and he would later refer to 'this long disease my life'. Because he was Catholic, he was barred from attending university. But the brilliance of his mind shines through his writing, much of which is satirical – poking poisonous fun at all manner of targets. His long poem *The Dunciad* is a satire on the society of the time; *The Rape of the Lock* attacks much of the fatuous writing of the period; his *Essay on Man* takes the obsessions and pomposity of human beings apart, shred by shred. Pope does not make easy reading these days – and his use of the rhyming couplet can seem tightly-constrained and monotonous. But his ferocity in attacking his targets, and his power of language, can make him great fun. *(See p. 124)*

William Trevor (1928–)

William Trevor is one of our greatest short story writers. Some of his work is set firmly in his native Ireland, but he is equally at home creating settings in England, or Italy. A key theme in his work is the destruction of innocence – of the way marriage suppresses individuality, of faded hopes, of dreams gone wrong. He is a particularly shrewd observer of women characters. His novels are also wonderful: you might try the disturbing *Children of Dynmouth* (1976), in which a psychotic teenager menaces a retirement resort by the sea. *(See p. 10)*

Virginia Woolf (1882–1941)

Virginia Woolf was plagued by mental illness throughout her life and which drove her finally to suicide. She believed strongly that modern fiction should faithfully capture the reality of real life. She therefore describes with painstaking details the perceptions and feelings of her characters, showing the world from their point of view. Her work undoubtedly changed the direction of the novel. *(See p. 107)*

Literary Contexts

Understanding the Context

When studying a text for coursework or examination, we can easily treat the text as if it exists in complete isolation. It can seem so important to us that we forget to think about how the text might have been perceived when it was written.

Yet texts grow out of a context, and the National Curriculum and GCSE syllabuses all require students to learn more about the different factors that make up this context.

In looking at a text we might ask:
- What was happening to the writer at this time? (Biographical perspective)
- What was happening in society at this time? (Social and historical perspectives)
- What were people's attitudes to texts like this at the time it was written? (Cultural perspective)
- How was language used at this time? (Stylistic perspective)

Let us consider some examples of how looking at context can give us a fuller understanding of a text.

Biographical Perspective

Knowing about the life and background of a writer can help us to respond more fully to the text – for example, knowing about Wilfred Owen's background, his relationships, and ambitions can add extra meaning to his poems of the First World War.

Social and Historical Perspective

Knowing about what life was like at the time a text was written can help us to understand the writer's portrayal – for example, knowing about the political system of the eighteenth century gives us greater insight into the satire and jokes in Jonathan Swift's novel, *Gulliver's Travels*.

Cultural Perspective

Knowing about the reading habits of people in a certain period might help us to understand the way the text is constructed – for example, the monthly publication of instalments of Victorian novels explains why Charles Dickens' novels contain 'cliff-hangers' – to make readers eager to read the next instalment.

Stylistic Perspective

Knowing that in a certain period there were 'unwritten' rules about how language could be used helps us to explain the style of particular texts – for example, the notion that certain words were ideal for poetry and others were inappropriate helps us to understand the way vocabulary is used in some eighteenth-century poetry.

This unit explores some of the historical contexts you may encounter when studying literature. It includes:

- **The Age of Shakespeare**
- **The Augustan Period**
- **The Romantics**
- **The Victorian novel**
- **The First World War Poets**

Each section looks briefly at the society, the writers, and the language of the period by picking out some of its key features. It then includes a sample text for you to explore in more detail.

The Age of Shakespeare

Shakespeare is undoubtedly the most famous writer in English. Because every student of English Literature has to 'do' Shakespeare at Key Stage 3, GCSE and A-level, the emphasis has been on the need to know a specific text for the exam. Little time has been devoted to the life of Shakespeare himself, or the period when he was writing.

The Society

It was an age of astonishing discoveries. America was discovered, as sailing ships set off on bold voyages to find new worlds. Life at home was changing: potatoes, tomatoes, and tobacco were first seen in Britain. Plague was still a major hazard, and London theatres would regularly close during the summer months and their companies head out on tour into the provinces to avoid disease. It was also an age of cruelty and intrigue. Bear-baiting, public hangings, and other brutal punishments were all routine. In November 1605 during the state opening of Parliament, Guy Fawkes was arrested in the cellars below, attempting to blow up the House of Lords.

The Writer

William Shakespeare (1564–1616)
We know surprisingly little of the details of Shakespeare's life. In a public profession (playwright and actor) he has managed to leave few personal clues. We know that he was born in Stratford upon Avon and that his

father was a wealthy glove-maker. We believe that Shakespeare attended the local grammar school, and later married Anne Hathaway. He had three children – Susannah and the twins, Judith and Hamnet. Shakespeare joined a London theatre company and was sufficiently well-known by 1592 to be called an 'upstart crow' by a rival playwright – probably for his part in writing *Henry VI*.

From then on he wrote some early comedies (*The Comedy of Errors, Two Gentlemen of Verona*, and *The Taming of the Shrew*), followed by some gory tragedies (*Titus Andronicus* and *Richard III*). His success made him the resident playwright with the influential acting company, the Lord Chamberlain's Men. The success of his plays – *The Merchant of Venice, Romeo and Juliet, Henry V* brought him wealth as well as popularity: in 1597 he bought New Place, one of Stratford's finest houses.

During his mature years – especially 1598 to 1605 – Shakespeare wrote his most famous, and most complex, plays –*Twelfth Night, Macbeth, Othello*. Haunted by sadness and a feeling of the treachery of power and status, we wonder what was happening in Shakespeare's own life which led to such an outpouring of disturbances. We suspect that the early death of his only son, Hamnet, must have deeply affected him. His later years were less spectacularly creative, and he appears to have retired to Stratford in 1613, where he died in 1616.

The Language

No one has had more impact on the language than William Shakespeare. Sometimes simple, sometimes astonishingly complex, his use of words shows us the thoughts and feelings of characters from 400 years ago (see Unit 5, pages 53–67). His jokes – an obsession with puns (word-play) have travelled least well down the centuries: many theatre productions try to cut them altogether. But his other gifts allow us to view people from another age as if they were alive today – explaining, perhaps, the success of modern Shakespeare film adaptations which show how relevant the plays can seem today.

Consider this example from one of Shakespeare's darkest, most unnerving plays, *Measure for Measure*. A new ruler has taken over a country, and he is determined to sort out its crime and poor morality. The audience will soon learn that he is as corrupt as those he condemns. As a result, Claudio has been sentenced to death for having unlawful sex with his fiancee. His sister Isabella, a nun, is here to wish him farewell … and Claudio sees an opportunity for her to help save his life …

....

Measure for Measure: Act 3, Scene 1

Isabella: What says my brother?

Claudio:	Death is a fearful thing.
Isabella:	And a shamed life a hateful.
Claudio:	Aye, but to die, and go we know not where,
	To lie in cold obstruction and to rot;
	This sensible warm motion to become
	A kneaded clod; and the delighted spirit
	To bathe in fiery floods, or to reside
	In thrilling region of thick-ribbed ice,
	To be imprisoned in the viewless winds
	And blown with restless violence round about
	The pendent world; or to be worse than worst
	Of those that lawless and in certain thought
	Imagine howling, 'tis too horrible.
	The weariest and most loathed worldly life
	That age, ache, penury, and imprisonment
	Can lay on nature is a paradise
	To what we fear of death.
Isabella:	Alas, alas.
Claudio:	Sweet sister, let me live.
	What sin you do to save a brother's life,
	Nature dispenses with the deed so far
	That it becomes a virtue.
Isabella:	O you beast!
	O faithless coward! O dishonest wretch!
	Wilt thou be made a man out my vice?
	Is't not a kind of incest to take life
	From thine own sister's shame? What should I think?
	Heaven shield my mother played my father fair,
	For such a warped slip of wilderness
	Ne'er issued from his blood. Take my defiance.
	Die, perish. Might but my bending down
	Reprieve thee from thy fate, it should proceed,
	I'll pray a thousand prayers for thy death,
	No word to save thee.
Claudio:	Nay, hear me Isabel.
Isabella:	O, fie, fie, fie!
	Thy sin's not accidental, but a trade.
	Mercy to thee would prove itself a bawd,
	'Tis best that thou diest quickly. GOING
Claudio:	O hear me, Isabella.

Activity

1 What is it that Claudio so fears about death?
2 How does he make death seem a horrifying prospect?
3 How does he try to persuade Isabella to help him?
4 How would you describe her reaction?
5 How does the language of the extract seem typical or untypical of Shakespeare, based on any other plays of his you have read?

The Augustans

The Society

At the end of the seventeenth century – a century after Shakespeare's birth – something seemed to happen in Britain, and a new mood of confidence can be felt. Daily life remained difficult and grim for many. The English Civil War (1626–49) had turned families against each other, as battles broke out between those supporting the King (Cavaliers) and those supporting Parliament (the Roundheads). A new king was installed in 1660; then the Plague swept through London; then, as if purging the city of this vicious disease, came the Great Fire of London in 1666. Relative calm seemed to follow. There was a growth of interest in writing – the first daily newspaper (*The Daily Current*) began in London in 1702; arguably the first novel, *Robinson Crusoe* was written by Daniel Defoe in 1719. But perhaps the dominant form of literature was poetry, which was used to entertain and amuse, but also to attack beliefs and attitudes of the time.

It was a time of artistic success – great painters like Thomas Gainsborough (1727–88) were showing landscapes where people were in perfect harmony with nature. Harmony and balance were the key features of the period.

The Writers

The dominant poets were John Dryden (1631–1700) and Alexander Pope (1688–1744), whose language was tightly-controlled and yet brilliantly flexible. Their poetry, like some of the prose writing of the period, is classed as satire: writing which pokes bitter fun at the people and attitudes of their day. Writing like this could seem general and public on the surface, whilst making personal attacks on specific people underneath. Some of these attacks are little short of outrageous.

Early novelists include Daniel Defoe (1660–1731), a former journalist, and Henry Fielding (1707–54), a would-be playwright who was banned from writing for the theatre because he had offended the Government. He turned instead to novels, writing stories about likeable and very human central characters, such as the hero of *Tom Jones*.

Language

Augustan poetry has a surface feeling of complete calm and order. Look at the rhyming couplets: they share the same rhythm; the rhyme feels reassuring and unchallenging; the vocabulary is unlikely to shock anyone and yet the subject-matter of many of the poems did shock (either because they make veiled attacks on people who are famous, or because

of the way they describe human beings – as little more than beasts).
Jonathan Swift here describes his vision of *The Day of Judgement*, when humans face God to explain the lives they have led.

The Day of Judgement

With a whirl of thought oppressed,
I sunk from reverie to rest.
A horrid vision seized my head,
I saw the graves give up their dead!
Jove, armed with terrors, bursts the skies,
And thunder roars and lightning flies!
Amazed, confused, its fate unknown,
The world stands trembling at his throne!
While each pale sinner hangs his head,
Jove, nodding, shook the heavens, and said:
'Offending race of human kind,
By nature, reason, learning, blind;
You who through frailty, stepped aside;
And you who never fell through pride:
You who different sects have shammed,
And come to see each other damned;
(So some folk told you, but they knew
No more of Jove's designs than you)
The world's mad business now is o'er,
And I resent these pranks no more.
I to such blockheads set my wit!
I damn such fools! – Go, go, you're bit.'

Activity

1   What does Swift see on the Day of Judgement?
2   What picture does he present of human beings?
3   Which words in the poem show his strength of feeling?
4   What would you say was his main message in the poem?
5   What surprises are there in the vocabulary?
6   What hints of satire are there in the poem – who or what might Swift be attacking?

The Romantics

The Society

By the end of the eighteenth century important new ideas were reaching Britain from the continent – ideas which placed more emphasis on the feelings and rights of the individual and less on conforming to society. 'Romanticism' (with a capital R) came to mean the celebration of feelings, personal individualism, and nature – rather than being linked to 'romantic' love as it is today.

This was, after all, an age of revolutions – most significantly in France where people appeared for a short time to have overturned centuries of tradition by deposing the King. Revolution of a different kind was to change Britain for good: the arrival of industrial processes led to huge population shifts, as people moved from the countryside to the squalor of unprepared towns and cities in search of new work.

Canals and railways opened Britain up. Factories and mills flourished from 1790 onwards. Gas lamps (first used in 1792) began to transform the streets of cities. By 1806 the British cotton industry employed 90,000 factory workers. And with industrial progress came squalor and exploitation: women, men, and children working lengthy hours in intolerable conditions; children sent down mines and up chimneys. The Devil himself appeared to some people to have taken over.

The Writers

William Blake (1757–1827) wrote poems which did not attempt to control the anger he felt. Looking at London's streets he notes marks of weakness, marks of woe, as if all humans beings are being crushed into evil submission and suffering. And just as urban life appears to become darker, so nature takes on greater significance. William Wordsworth (1770–1850) in particular celebrates the capacity of nature to fill humans with wonder, to teach us more about ourselves. The best-known Romantics, Wordsworth, Samuel Taylor Coleridge (1772–1834), John Keats (1795–1821), and Percy Bysshe Shelley (1792–1822), each write with an emphasis on the power of the human imagination, the importance of freedom, and the overwhelming power of nature.

Mary Shelley's (1797–1851) novel *Frankenstein* (1818) is perhaps the strongest reminder from the Romantic period of the dangers of industrialization – creating monsters we cannot control, and of dabbling with nature.

The Language

The language of the Romantic poets contrasts fairly sharply with their ·

Augustan predecessors. The desire for balance and harmony, with the tightly-controlled forms of poetry, is abandoned. The emphasis is on writing in the style which best suits the meaning. And the language is altogether more personal, more emotional, and frequently more spiritual. Read Wordsworth describing a childhood memory of going into the woods to collect hazelnuts. He describes the scene in highly charged language, crossing beds of matted fern, and tangled thicket to arrive at one dear nook unvisited. Here, in this virgin scene, a place never before visited by humans, he launches a wild, unexpected attack on nature:

Nutting

…Perhaps it was a bower beneath whose leaves
the violets of five seasons re-appear
and fade, unseen by any human eye;
Where fairy water-breaks do murmur on
Forever; and I saw the sparkling foam,
And – with my cheek on one of those green stones
That, fleeced with moss, under the shady trees,
Lay round me, scattered like a flock of sheep –
I heard the murmur and the murmuring sound,
In that sweet mood when pleasure loves to pay
Tribute to ease; and, of its joy secure,
The heart luxuriates with indifferent things,
Wasting its kindliness on stocks and stones,
And on the vacant air. Then up I rose,
And dragged to earth both branch and bough, with crash
And merciless ravage: and the shady nook
Of hazels, and the green and mossy bower,
Deformed and sullied, patiently gave up
Their quiet being: and, unless I now
Confound my present feelings with the past,
Ere from the mutilated bower I turned
Exulting, rich beyond the wealth of kings,
I felt a sense of pain when I beheld
The silent trees, and saw the intruding sky. –
Then, dearest Maiden, move along these shades
In gentleness of heart; with gentle hand
Touch – for there is a spirit in the woods.

1 The poem begins with a picture of the tranquil wood. How does Wordsworth suggest that the place is special?
2 What image do you get of the mossy stones *scattered like a flock of sheep*?
3 How does the wood respond when the poet begins to attack it?
4 What different emotions does he feel during the extract?
5 At the end Wordsworth addresses *dearest Maiden*. Who do you think this is and what is he asking of her?
6 How does Wordsworth's vocabulary feel different from Jonathan Swift's in the last spread?

The Victorian Era

The Society

The Victorian era (1837–1901) was a period of huge social changes. It begins with some dark legacies of industrialization: urban poverty, child labour, slavery, and the suppression of the rights of women. Yet it is also a period of reform and progress. In 1828 there had been 26 miles of railway in Britain. By 1844 there were 2,236 miles. Medical discoveries, such as the smallpox vaccination which was made compulsory in 1853, transformed life-expectancy in Britain. In 1870 the Education Act introduced statutory education for all, a huge milestone on the road to literacy and an escape for many from the poverty trap.

The Writers

Poetry was influential and often powerful, rooted in the Romantic tradition. Alfred Lord Tennyson (1809–1892) looked back to history for inspiration, to the legends of King Arthur, whilst Robert Browning (1812–1889) and Elizabeth Barrett Browning (1806–1861) made poetry more private, exploring relationships between men and women. Poetry of the period shows these strong oppositions: Tennyson writing of grand, public themes, whilst others looked inward towards private emotions, for example the work of the deeply reclusive Emily Dickinson (1830–86). But literature in this period was dominated by the novel, a form which gained huge popular appeal thanks to the growth of lending libraries and subscription schemes. These made it possible for ordinary people to read books which they could not always afford to buy at once. The publication schedule, a new episode of the serial each month, led to complex plots, vast collections of characters and to storylines which would build to regular climaxes in order to keep the reader hanging on for the next instalment.

The master of the popular novel was undoubtedly Charles Dickens

(1812–70). His working pattern was to devote two weeks of each month to producing the following month's instalment. He wrote on standard size paper so that he could work out precisely how much he had to write for the next episode. Just occasionally he miscalculated and had to dash to the printers to cut or add text. Sometimes his timetabling was also out. One day he overheard a woman in a stationer's shop asking for the next instalment of David Copperfield. The assistant said it would be available at the end of the month. Dickens panicked. He knew that he had not yet written a word.

The Language

The popularity of the novel today owes much to the Victorian novel, because the great writers of the period used such a range of styles to express their meanings. Dickens used comedy and melodrama, retelling memorable stories with a host of often eccentric characters. George Eliot (1819–80) used more reflective language. Her novels were concerned with the role of the individual within society. Thomas Hardy (1840–1928), writing at the end of the century, changed the focus again, presenting central characters who lived lives in spite of the society around them. Society and fate frequently seem to conspire against Hardy's characters – giving us a style which is far removed from the exuberant eccentricities of Dickens' lighter moments.

Look at this extract from Hardy's novel *Tess of the D'Urbervilles*. The tranquillity of the countryside is suddenly fractured by the appearance of a new-fangled threshing machine, and the threatening figure who accompanies it. Thus Hardy shows the effect of industrialization on rural life.

Tess of the D'Urbervilles

It is the threshing of the last wheat-rick at Flintcomb-Ash Farm. The dawn of the March morning is singularly inexpressive, and there is nothing to show where the eastern horizon lies. Against the twilight rises the trapezoidal top of the stack, which has stood forlornly here through the washing and bleaching of the wintry weather.

When Izz Huett and Tess arrived at the scene of operations only a rustling denoted that others had preceded them; to which, as the light increased, there were presently added the silhouettes of two men on the summit. They were busily 'unhaling' the rick, that is stripping off the thatch before beginning to throw down the sheaves; and while this was in progress Izz and Tess, with the other women-workers, in their whity-brown pinners, stood waiting and shivering, Farmer Groby having insisted upon their being on the spot thus early to get the job over if possible by the end of the day. Close under the eaves of the stack, and as yet barely visible, was the red tyrant that the women had come

to serve – a timber-framed construction, with straps and wheels appertaining – the threshing-machine which, whilst it was going, kept up a despotic demand upon the endurance of their muscles and nerves.

A little way off there was another indistinct figure; this one black, with a sustained hiss that spoke of strength very much in reserve. The long chimney running up beside the ash-tree, and the warmth which radiated from the spot, explained without the necessity of much daylight that here was the engine which was to act as the *primum mobile* of this little world. By the engine stood a dark motionless being, a sooty and grimy embodiment of tallness, in a sort of trance, with a heap of coals by his side: it was the engine man. The isolation of his manner and colour lent him the appearance of a creature from Tophet, who had strayed into the pellucid smokelessness of this region of yellow grain and pale soil, with which he had nothing in common, to amaze and discompose its aborigines.

What he looked he felt. He was in the agricultural world, but not of it. He served fire and smoke; these denizens of the fields served vegetation, weather, frost, and sun. He travelled with his engine from farm to farm, from county to county, for as yet the steam threshing-machine was itinerant in this part of Wessex. He spoke in a strange northern accent; his thoughts being turned inwards upon himself, his eye on his iron charge, hardly perceiving the scenes around him, and caring for them not at all: holding only strict necessary intercourse with the natives, as if some ancient doom compelled him to wander here against his will in the service of his Plutonic master. The long strap which ran from the driving wheel of his engine to the red thresher under the rick was the sole tie-line between agriculture and him.

While they uncovered the sheaves he stood apathetic beside his portable repository of force, round whose hot blackness the morning air quivered. He had nothing to do with preparatory labour. His fire was waiting incandescent, his steam was at high pressure, in a few seconds he could make the long strap move at an invisible velocity. Beyond its extent the environment might be corn, straw, or chaos; it was all the same to him. If any of the autochthonous idlers asked him what he called himself, he replied shortly, 'an engineer'.

● ●

Activity

1 Which negative words can you find to describe the machine?
2 Hardy hints that there is something devilish about the machine and its owner – what clues can you find?
3 What effect does the machine have on the women?
4 What do you notice about the vocabulary and sentence structure of the extract?

The First World War Poets

The Society

In 1914 Britain was a hugely different place from 100 years earlier. In 1814 John Macadam was about to introduce his system of using crushed stones to create roads. There were not yet horse-drawn buses, let alone cars. By 1914 towns and cities had properly-constructed roads which already, at times, seemed clogged with cars. The American Ford Motor Company produced its Model 'T' design which would go on to sell 15 million. The London Underground system (begun in 1884) whisked people beneath London – a huge feat of engineering.

People who could afford it had running water in their houses. Streets were often lit by streetlights and were altogether cleaner. Medical progress in the past 100 years had transformed health, so that most people could expect to live healthy lives.

All of these advances seemed like huge progress. But by 1914 a series of political events, concluding with the assassination of Archduke Ferdinand of Serbia led the states of Europe to topple into war. It was a war that would change the world for ever – more brutal and more costly in human lives than anything that had gone before.

The new trench warfare meant that little progress was made – the two opposing sides faced each other across No-Man's-Land, strewn with a new invention from the USA for controlling cattle – barbed wire. At night when the attacks began, soldiers were shot at or shelled by the enemy, choked, in drifting gas, or tangled helplessly in the barbed wire. By the end of the War around eight and a half million had been killed, and 21 million wounded. In almost any town or village in Western Europe there are memorials to the war's victims, ordinary people whose lives were lost in the world's worst war.

The Writers

Our understanding of what made the First World War such a vicious, brutal affair comes largely from the writers who were there. Isaac Rosenberg (1890–1918) was a poet and artist killed in battle in France. His body was never recovered. His poems are characterized by their harsh, bleak language. Siegfried Sassoon (1886–1967) came from a comfortable background and won admiration (and the nickname 'mad Jack') for his courage in battle. His poetry is especially critical of the incompetence of the commanders. He writes with a fierce bitterness. Wilfred Owen (1893–1918) is probably the best-known of the war poets. He already had a passion for poetry, and many of his early poems have echoes of the Romantic themes and style of John Keats. More memorably than any other writer Owen has shown us the individual sufferings and horrors of the First World War.

The Language

When critics list the most influential poems of the twentieth century most would have *The Wasteland*, by T.S. Eliot (1888–1965) high on their list. It is a disturbing and difficult poem because it is so fragmented, so hard to piece together. It probably could not have been written without the influence of the War Poets, who changed the English Language and poetry for ever by forcing it to confront, through verse, some of the horrors of the trenches. A decade before Georgian poetry had been elegant, emotional and, for many readers today, full of sickly emotion. The war poets made language hard, descriptive and brutally emotional. Here, as an example, is Siegfried Sassoon's poem, *Attack*, written in 1917.

Attack

At dawn the ridge emerges massed and dun
In wild purple of the glow'ring sun,
Smouldering through spouts of drifting smoke that shroud
The menacing scarred slope; and one by one,
Tanks creep and topple forward to the wire.
The barrage roars and lifts. Then, clumsily bowed
With bombs and guns and shovels and battle-gear,
Men jostle and climb to meet the bristling fire.
Lines of grey, muttering faces, masked with fear.
They leave their trenches, going over the top,
While time ticks blank and busy on their wrists,
And hope, with furtive eyes and grappling fists,
Flounders in mud. O Jesus, make it stop!

Activity

1 What picture of the battlefield does Sassoon create?
2 What does he suggest about the men when he says that they are *clumsily bowed with bombs and guns and shovels and battle-gear*?
3 What image does he create in *time ticks blank and busy on their wrists*?
4 What happens to the men?
5 How does Sassoon show his anger at what happens?

Acknowledgements

The publisher would like to thank the following for permission to reproduce photographs:

Popperfoto: p 15; Bridgeman Art Library/Cecil Higgins Art Gallery, Bedford: p 21; Oxford Scientific Films/Lon Lauber: p 28; Popperfoto: pp 45,46; Mary Evans Picture Library: p 49; Donald Cooper/Photostage: p 56; Ronald Grant Archive: pp 65, 67; J Allan Cash: pp 69, 71; Mary Evans Picture Library: p 75; Donald Cooper/Photostage: pp 95, 98; Bruce Coleman/P Clement: p 101; Mary Evans Picture Library: p 110; Bridgeman Art Library/Brooklyn Museum of Art: p 114; Popperfoto: pp 120, 123; Bridgeman Art Library/Agnew & Sons, London: p 125; J Allan Cash: p 127; Mary Evans Picture Library (centre): p 132; J Allan Cash: p 135.

The illustrations are by:

Gerry Ball c/o Eikon Ltd pp 26, 93, 114; Tim Clarey pp 12, 23, 78, 79; Martin Cottam pp 9, 90; Chris Duggan p 44; Rosamund Fowler pp 74, 103; Zhenya Matysiak pp 59, 105; Ian Mitchell pp 6, 20, 32, 43, 53, 68, 89, 99,118, 136; Lyn O'Neill p 40; Brian Pedley p 58; Mark Robertson pp 10, 73, 81, 83, 86, 88; Sarah Young pp 61, 98. Cover illustration by Gary Thompson Studio including photo of Grace Nichols by Fanny Dubes and photos of Shakespeare and Nelson Mandela by Corbis Uk Ltd.

The following material is reprinted here by permission of the copyright holders:

David Almond: 'Lucy Blue' first published in A Kind of Heaven by David Almond (Iron Press, 1997), and notes about writing short stories, both by permission of the author.
Isaac Asimov: extracts from 'Cal' and 'Kid Brother' reprinted from Gold (The Final Science Fiction Selection, 1990).
W H Auden: 'Look Stranger at this Island Now' reprinted from Collected Poems edited by Edward Mendelson, by permission of the publishers, Faber & Faber Ltd.
Marjorie Barnard: extracts from 'The Lottery' reprinted from The Persimmom Tree and Other Stories (Virago, 1985), by permission of the author, care of Curtis Brown (Australia).
Samuel Beckett: extract reprinted from opening of Waiting for Godot (1956) by permission of the publishers, Faber & Faber Ltd.
E Kamau Brathwaite: 'Limbo' reprinted from The Arrivants (OUP, 1973) by permission of Oxford University Press.
Christopher Burns: opening of 'Mrs Pulsaka' reprinted from Duncan Minshull (ed): The Best of BBC Radio's Recent Short Fiction (Coronet/Hodder & Stoughton), by permission of Hodder & Stoughton Ltd.
Angela Carter: extract from 'The Company of Wolves' reprinted from The Company of Wolves (Chatto & Windus, 1996) by permission of Rogers, Coleridge & White Ltd, 20 Powis Mews, London W11 1JN.
Anton Chekhov: extract reprinted from opening of The Shooting Party translated by A E Chamot, revised by Julian Symons (Deutsch, 1964, 1986).
CLEO 11 massager magazine advertisement used by permission of The Kaymar Group Ltd.
Coldseal Windows radio advertisement used by permission of the author and Coldseal Ltd.
Country Cottages Ireland advertisement used by permission of the Holiday Cottages Group Ltd.
David Crystal: extract from a letter reprinted from The English Language (Pelican, 1988), by permission of Penguin Books Ltd.
Carol Ann Duffy: 'Words, Wide Night' reprinted from The Other Country (Anvil Press Poetry, 1990),by permission of the publisher.
Glevum Windows press advertisement used by permission of Glevum Windows.
Seamus Heaney: 'The Otter' reprinted from Field Work (1979) and 'The Follower' reprinted from Death of a Naturalist (1966) by permission of the publishers, Faber & Faber Ltd.
Christopher Hope: opening of 'My Good Fairy' reprinted from Duncan Minshull (ed): The Best of BBC Radio's Recent Short Fiction (Coronet/Hodder & Stoughton), by permission of Hodder & Stoughton Ltd.
Ernest Hemingway: opening of 'The Killers' reprinted from In the Snows of Kilimanjaro and Other Stories (Jonathan Cape, 1963).
Hutchinson Dictionary of Science: copyright © Helicon Publishing Ltd, 1993, extracts reprinted by permission of the publisher, all rights reserved.
Henrik Ibsen: extracts reprinted from The Doll's House (Methuen Students' Edition 1974) by permission of Methuen.
The Independent: article by Charles Arthur, 'Kraken or Tree Trunk? Mystery Blob from the Deep Confounds the Experts' reprinted from The Independent, 10.1.98, by permission of Independent Newspapers (UK) Ltd. Accompanying photograph by Rick Eaves reproduced by permission of Solo Syndication Ltd.
Kitekat™ television commercial script used by permission of Pedigree Masterfoods, Mars UK Ltd. KITEKAT is a registered trademark.
Doris Lessing: opening of 'The Other Woman' reprinted from A Man and Two Women, copyright ©1963 Doris Lessing, by permission of Jonathan Clowes Ltd, London, on behalf of Doris Lessing.
Roger McGough: 'The Identification' reprinted from GIG (Cape) by permission of the Peters Fraser & Dunlop Group Ltd.
Arthur Miller: extract from Death of a Salesman, copyright © 1949 by Arthur Miller, and extract from The Crucible, copyright © 1952, 1953 by Arthur Miller, reprinted by permission of the author c/o Rogers, Coleridge & White Ltd, 20 Powis Mews, London W11 1JN in association with International Creative Management Inc.
Liam O'Flaherty: extracts from 'The Wounded Cormorant' reprinted from The Short Stories of Liam O'Flaherty (Cape) by permission of the Peters Fraser & Dunlop Group Ltd.
Siegfried Sassoon: 'The Attack' reprinted from The War Poems edited by Rupert Hart-Davis (Faber, 1983), copyright © Siegfried Sassoon, by permission of George Sassoon, care of the Barbara Levy Literary Agency.
Grace Nichols: 'Island Man' reprinted from The Fat Black Woman's Poems (Virago, 1984), copyright © Grace Nichols 1984, by permission of Curtis Brown Ltd, London on behalf of the author.
William Shakespeare: extracts reprinted from The Complete Oxford Shakespeare, by permission of Oxford University Press.
Penelope Shuttle: 'Downpour' reprinted from The Orchard Upstairs (OUP) by permission of David Higham Associates Ltd.
John Steinbeck: opening extract reprinted from The Grapes of Wrath (Heinemann, 1939) by permission of Random House UK Ltd.
The Sun: article by Nick Parker, 'I peeped out from sheet ..', and article, 'Roof landed in Bedroom', both reprinted from The Sun, 9.1.98, by permission of News International.
Anne Stevenson: 'The Marriage' reprinted from The Collected Poems of Anne Stevenson 1955-1995 (OUP, 1996) by permission of Oxford University Press.
Graham Swift: extract reprinted from Last Orders (Picador, 1996) by permission of Macmillan and A.P. Watt Ltd on behalf of the author..
Margaret Thatcher: Gala Birthday Tribute to President Ronald Reagan (1994), by permission of Margaret Thatcher.
William Trevor: opening of 'Miss Smith' reprinted from Collected Stories (Bodley Head, 1992).
Fay Weldon: extract from 'Weekend' reprinted from Watching Me, Watching You (Hodder & Stoughton, 1981), copyright © Fay Weldon 1981, by permission of Curtis Brown Ltd, on behalf of the author.

Although every effort has been made to trace and contact copyright holders before publication this has not always been possible. If notified, the publisher will be pleased to rectify any errors or omissions at the earliest opportunity.